Treading or

My life with my au

By

Christine Breakey

ISBNs:
Paperback: 978-1-80227-137-9
eBook: 978-1-80227-138-6

Dedication

For Rhiannon and Carys:
my past; my present and my future.

You are my pride and my joy.

I love you more than words can say.

Contents

Foreword

Reading Christine's book led me to many 'aha' moments. Having come from 'Welsh roots' (my maternal grandparents & great grandparents were Welsh) I recognise aspects of this unique story and find myself understanding and agreeing to so many mirrored reflections. Like Christine, we lived not far from The Severn Bridge (the bridge that connects Wales to England) when I was a youngster (between the ages of 4-17). Unlike Christine though, we lived on the other side, the English side of that same bridge. One's heritage, whatever it is, impacts our lives in various ways and intergenerational trauma will carry scars impacting our responses to a vast number of perceived societal and family interactions. Christine's story about her Mum's autism and how that played out in both her Mum's nuclear family and, later in Christine's family, with her Mum, Dad and sister, then with the promises Christine made to herself about her own parenting style, are peculiar to them. However, they also house aspects of family life that we all might identify with. Not because we all have autism in our families but, because we come from families where secrets abide, and lives are influenced.

Much of the beginnings of 'Treading on Eggshells' echo memories from my own experience of growing up during the same era and in a family dogged by secrets. I also lived with a mother, undiagnosed formally as autistic, but autistic I'm sure she was. I can also identify with Christine's tug of war over wanting to present 'autism' in an appropriate light, while recognizing the relational 'trauma' she experienced growing up. But, unlike Christine, I'm sad to say, I don't think I achieved a state of 'forgiveness' when it comes to my own mother, who died aged 98 in 2018.

We know from various research findings that autism is majorly genetic. I am 'Mum' (OK, a Man Mum) to our 3 autistic off-spring and we have 3 autistic grand-children. 'Keep it in the family' we frequently joke! I know being autistic is precious to us but the fact that we joke about it shows the depth of stigma autism still carries.

Christine's Mum knew the protection of a family that covered for her, but they did not understand her. Christine's father was a trouper through and through, a man of integrity and commitment who recognised the need to relinquish control to his wife, in order to keep the family intact. But, like Christine's grandparents, he neither understood his wife's constant mental anguish or was able to help her find the appropriate tools she needed to negotiate everyday life. Instead, the family lived by presenting one 'face' to the outside world and another 'face' at home. Christine didn't know that her family life was dysfunctional. To her, this was normal. I had to smile when I read it was common to have bread and butter with canned rice pudding, or a can of fruit salad as a main meal! I knew this experience too. In fact, some days when I feel a need for comfort I turn towards that bread thickly spread with Anchor butter and open a tin of Ambrosia creamed rice!

The sparsity of home furnishings in Christine's home growing up, the lack of carpeting throughout and the need for her Mum to buy expensive clothing from a catalogue (rather than face to face from shop people) was made all the easier due to the nature of the practices of the time. I'm not surprised she incurred debts that took time to reveal themselves and time to pay off. Christine was born just seven years after World War 2 and poverty was rife, yet the need to present outwardly to the wider community as if one was 'better off' and the pull for status was one way to try to avoid stigma. Christine's Mum would have been unwittingly drawn to ways that camouflaged her outer life. It was only during extreme stress, paranoia, mis-belief and perceived chaos that her Mum moved beyond her ability to contain herself and all havoc let loose. This is all too common in autism in our present day. Many have felt pushed into hiding their true selves, to morph and mask who they are in order to keep safe, 'fit in' and avoid being bullied. It will only be as we change our responses toward autistic individuals, choose to live our lives without pretense as autistic people and bravely declare our needs and our rights, that we will have a hope of changing this.

Neurodiversity, like biodiversity (all life on earth), simply means 'all neurotypes'. I don't use the term neurodivergent divergent to describe autism or being autistic. I am autistic and autism describes my neurotype. Neurodivergent means to diverge away from the usual. Neurodiversity encompasses ALL neurotypes... we are all usual and all part of neurodiversity. I use divergent to talk about being of diverse abilities and not confined to one group. Like in the Film 'Divergent': https://en.wikipedia.org/wiki/The_Divergent_Series

If we are to contribute to the removal of stigma we need to own our autism, and that of intergenerational consequence. As Christine so rightly describes in this revealing and courageous book, it's not enough to have 'autism acceptance' within our ranks. We need to move several steps beyond this towards actively embracing and actioning understanding so it takes on a living form and is naturally expressed across the lifespan.

It's likely we all know 'someone' in our past, whether from school years or within our own families, and the explanation for their 'challenging behaviour' might have been that they lived and moved among a population of challenges they had no way of navigating. This meant they often expressed their frustration, pain and fear through anger at self or at others. It's all too easy to pass judgement upon their responses and not recognise the challenges they faced. If you took language literally; if 'jokes' and teasing went 'over your head'; if the only way you could navigate your days was by staying with a routine and scheduling your work load as well as only working within your area of interest (with Christine's Mum it was like this with numbers and her daily need for sameness); if 'other people' made little sense to you and their actions caused you anxiety, then it's clear your responses to being part of the world we all live in, might be impulsive and angry. Christine's Mum was an intelligent woman. Autism is no respecter of persons and one's IQ does not prevent autism. In fact, if you are able to speak and understand as a person of average or above IQ, you have the gift of insight without the ability to affect how autism impacts your life. Sometimes having such insight only serves to increase one's daily trauma in a world that does not accommodate difference. This scenario applies to around 70-80% of autistic individuals.

Many autistic individuals who are alternative communicators (who don't use speech) are intellectually able, but often they are overlooked because their autism, sensory needs and often dyspraxic disposition causes them to behave in ways seen as not socially acceptable. Why is this? It's because we have failed them. We have failed to stand up for autistic difference; we have failed to give them the tools they need to enable them to 'successfully live among us'. My friend Tim Chan knows this only too well. See: My Travels with Autism at: https://www.youtube.com/watch?v=T_wX8VgcGp4

As with Christine, I welcomed the opportunity to parent my own children differently. Their autism is different for each one of them as are their personalities. My Mum used to say: 'I treat you all the same'. My response, internally though, was to say to myself 'but, we are not all the same so we need to be treated as individuals, with individual needs and so on'. Life should be about equity and treating people with impartiality and fairness. I know this can be hard to achieve, especially when we don't feel treated fairly ourselves. Christine managed to grasp this concept and turn away from her own hurt to see the possible reasons for her Mum's behaviour. Its only as we see beyond the immediate and past the 'behaviour' that we give ourselves a chance to reach an understanding. Forgiveness isn't a feeling, it's an act of our will. But, it will mean the need to turn away from the hurt and the injustice; walk away from it and leave it behind. Sometimes I think we may need to revisit this action several times before it solidifies and we can honestly say 'it's done'.

For my own life I see this as 'a work in progress'! Christine's journey to coming to terms with her Mum's autism and the reasons for it's impact upon her life could have left Christine bitter and resentful. She has every right to blame 'autism' for the lack of a warm and nurturing childhood. Yes, Christine's Dad did his best, but there was a side to him that could be rebellious, defiant and almost 'uncaring'… I could imagine that he too was the product of his time, generation, gender and possible autistic traits. But he would also have felt like he was pushing a wheelbarrow up hill and despite his love, loyalty and commitment to his wife and family, he would have known dark times and times of isolation. None of us are meant to live our lives in a bubble. We all need community. We all need connection. Christine chose to see beyond her own hurt and sought to unravel the puzzle that was her Mum. We are grateful! Had Christine not chosen to do so, this book would not have been written and we would not be benefiting from its insights. Learning from Christine's life story and relating it to our own is a good thing. Seeing even further though and pledging our commitment to bettering the lives of autistic 'others' as we work together, as a community, to enable us all to access the tools we each need to live the kind of life we can be proud of, is the only way forward.

Dr. Wenn B. Lawson (PhD)
CPsychol AFBPsS MAPS ASSW.

Preface

This book is written in honour of my autistic mother who, with my father succeeded in raising her two children in an environment which was at odds with her neurological type. It is also written to honour all autistic mothers who find themselves and their parenting criticised by the majority, or the dominant neurotype who are unable to reach a shared understanding of the joy of diversity: the diversity which is the very essence of humanity, nature and creation.

The book has been sixteen years in the thinking and one year in the writing: in 2005, when I was nearing the completion of writing *The Autism Spectrum and Further Education*, I told a friend that I already knew that my next book would be about my autistic mother and that it would be called '*Treading on Eggshells*': a title which would convey both the fragility and the strength of the relationship that I had with my autistic mother. I had no idea at that time that it would take me so long to write, or that the writing of it would present so many challenges or be so cathartic.

Everyone who knows me well, knows that autism is my special interest and my passion, and that working with autistic people has for many years been my profession.

They will know that I am passionate about using an 'inside-out approach' in my work, something that I learnt from Donna Williams (aka Polly Samuel), and that I am adamant that those who consider themselves to be part of the dominant neurotype, have a responsibility to find ways to connect, understand and empathise with those who's neurological make up is different to theirs. People who know me well, will also know that I love language and that I am determined that we should strive to use language in non-discriminatory ways, recognising that words are powerful, having the ability to encourage and build up as well as to discourage and destroy confidence and self-esteem. People who know me well, also know that I believe passionately that autistic people are the only experts in the field of autism and that their voice must be central to all our learning and teaching. Professionals working with autistic people have a responsibility to find ways to listen, absorb and apply our learning to our practice. Everyone who knows anything about me, will know that I am 'positive about autism': that I refuse to see it as a problem or a disorder; a condition which is defined by an absence of something, or a deficit in some area which makes autistic people less than whole. People who know me well, will know that I recognise that what are seen as the disabling aspects of autism do not arise from being autistic but are created, as they are with all disabilities, by a society which measures people against the 'norm' and discriminates against anyone who because of an impairment does not comply with that norm, and then does not accommodate those who do not. And finally: people who really know me well, will know that the reason that it took me sixteen years to write about my mother was precisely because of all of these things.

I wanted to write a book about my mother because I felt that autistic mothers are both ignored and marginalised, by society and that this is reflected in the autism literature. It is as if they don't exist, but most autistic girls grow up to be autistic women and many of them have and will become mothers and their experience of motherhood in a world which is not attuned to them, is fraught with many challenges, which are not recognised or talked about. There is pressure on all mothers to be perfect: perfect partners; perfect homemakers and perfect mothers, all whilst balancing the demands of work and a career, and they are blamed when they are unable to juggle all the demands that this brings. Within this culture there is a myth that autistic women do not make good mothers and many autistic mothers have had their children taken from them by society's institutions whose role is to protect the vulnerable. These same institutions have failed the autistic mother, because they have either not recognised that whilst autistic parenting may not follow societal norms, it is nevertheless a valid, and in many instances a better form of parenting for that child; or they have not supported the autistic mother in her relationships and haven't enabled her to learn how to nurture and care for her child, choosing instead to relocate that child into a neuro-typical family which often doesn't understand them or is unable to support the restoration and recovery of parental and familial relationships. I wanted to write this book because I thought that I had something to say and contribute to this subject as I think that my life could have taken a very different path, if it hadn't been for the fact that my mother's parenting difficulties were hidden from the wider society and its institutions by my father who stayed with my mother against all the odds, protecting and shielding both her and his daughters from the secrets of our home life. He was assisted in this by being part of a close-knit community who had known my mother since her birth and accepted her for who she was, without discrimination. Without him, my experience could have been quite different. I also wanted to write this book because I reached a point in my life when I was comfortable with who I was and I could see that despite their failings, my parents had done a 'good enough' job in raising me and that I am who I am, and I do what I do, because of them. No one can ask for more than that. I wanted to show those who are interested in autism, that autistic mothers (or indeed parents) could do this: they might do it differently, but they could do it well.

What then were the barriers to me writing this book, and why did it take me so long?

The truth, as painful as it is, is that I didn't like my mother for many years. I had labelled her as difficult, stubborn, aggressive, nasty, obsessive and violent and these labels prevented me from seeing the frightened, anxious, vulnerable and sensitive person who was hidden beneath them. These labels also prevented me from writing about her because the language that I used to describe her and my relationship with her, went against the very grain of my core beliefs about autism, and they forced me to recognise and confront an unconscious negative bias which I was ashamed of. This was shocking for me, and I was unable to find the words to write about my mother in a way which didn't conflict with my own deeply held positive beliefs about autism without first addressing my unconscious bias towards her. For me, this highlights the difference between autism awareness and autism acceptance: I had become aware that my mother was autistic in 2004 but that awareness was passive; it was something which I had and whilst it enabled me to understand her better, it didn't require me to alter my attitudes, thinking and behaviour towards her. It took time for me to work on my acceptance of her as autistic because to accept, unlike awareness, required an action from me. My acceptance of my mother's autism challenged me to do something about the words that I used to think about her and to describe her and as I have indicated, words are powerful and our choice and use of them influences and changes how we and others think. I am still continually challenged by this.

Familial relationships also meant that I had to consider others in the writing of this book. I wasn't able to write it when my parents and my sister were alive as it would have created immense hostility in a family which was as volatile as ours and I didn't want to be responsible for this. It has however still taken me another seven years since I have no longer had to consider this, for me to be able to put pen to paper.

For me, the problem with writing this book, after finding acceptance, was that I couldn't find a way into it without presenting my mother and her autism in a negative light. I recently read another autobiographical account of an autistic mother and daughter relationship and whilst it was highly praised for its painful, raw honesty, I found it to be an uncomfortable account of an autistic mother, who also suffered with mental ill health, and I didn't want my book to echo that discomfort. I was also painfully aware of the potential for viewing my mother's autism and her parenting skills out of context. Autism and Asperger Syndrome were unheard of when my mother was growing up in the 1930s, and her 1950s parenting style, whilst being different to what is currently viewed as acceptable, was not untypical of the period, but I continued to be anxious that I may misrepresent her in sharing this. I have come to realise that there is no judgement in this. It was what it was, at that point in time.

When discussing this and my fear of presenting both autism and my mother negatively with an autistic student who I support, she very kindly pointed out to me that my mother had done a good job in raising me, and that I was a good mother as a result. She helped me to see that my experience of my mother's mothering had equipped me with the skills which enabled me to devote most of my adult life to understanding and supporting other autistic people. This enabled me to see that the way into writing this book was through me and my family's history, and not through my mother, and this is the approach that I've taken.

This book is therefore an autobiographical account, written by the daughter of an autistic mother. It describes a personal journey of reconciliation and discovery, both of my mother's autism, but also of how that shaped me and equipped me with the skills which underpinned the whole of my professional life, as an autism practitioner. I found that I was unable to leave my father out of the story as he was central, as my mother's life-long companion and supporter, and also was a major influence in who I am and what I do. I also considered that my parents' inheritance and upbringings had a major impact, both genetically and socially, on them as people and parents, and subsequently on me as their child, so I have included chapters which give them and their relationship a broader context. Whilst the book focuses on my mother's autism and its impact on me, it has caused me to question my father's and my own neurology. I am undecided about my father, ultimately viewing him and my mother as the opposite sides of the same coin. Perhaps both were autistic? I have given insights to my own neurology throughout the book and have described it in more detail in the last chapter, but I make no claims to being autistic, having no diagnosis, nor feeling any need for one at this stage in my life, so I have intentionally left this for the reader to fathom and decide. I have also included some photographs as I feel they add a visual dimension and support to the written word.

Writing this book has required me to share uncomfortable, negative thoughts and emotions, from the time before my realisation that my mother was autistic, but I have tried my best to honour her and autism in a way which is honest, respectful and accepting. I hope more than anything that I have been successful in doing that, but I beg forgiveness for any failures that I may have made along the way.

This has been both a cathartic and painful path to tread but then treading on eggshells was never going to be comfortable or easy.

Please note that I have changed names of people in the text where there is a ned for confidentiality.

Acknowledgements

My thanks must first and foremost go to all of the autistic people (including my mother), who over the years have taught me everything that I know about autism, but my particular thanks go to Laura, whose encouragement, insight and support enabled me to find the way into writing this book and gave me the confidence to write and publish it.

My thanks also to my colleague Jamie, who read my draft and reassured me that my experience was worth writing about and that the book is an accurate representation of my core values and beliefs. His opinion and validation mean a great deal and without that I might not have considered publication.

And finally: my thanks to my husband Jim, who is my soul mate and the love of my life. He has patiently walked the last forty years of this journey with me, gently helping me to see with different eyes. My thanks to him also for his faith and belief in me, when I have doubted myself. His reading and honest feedback of each chapter has been an invaluable support. I couldn't have walked this journey without him. Nor would I have wanted to.

CHAPTER 1

Finding me

My life began in September 1972, at the age of nineteen. This may sound a bit odd, but for me, 1972 brought a freedom and release from the tight parental and community controls which stifled and suffocated the very essence of my existence. Like many Welsh teenagers in the 1970s, I was part of that first generation of working-class children to have the educational opportunities (funded by an attractive government grant), which enabled us to leave home and to either 'go to college' (as it was called back then), or to 'seek our fortunes' elsewhere. There was an atmosphere of social mobility and opportunity, and the expectation was that I should take advantage of that and leave home. It was in this context that I joined what seemed at the time to be the mass exodus of Welsh teenagers, heading to the great continually developing metropolis of London. An exodus which had been made more achievable by the opening of the Severn Bridge, just six years earlier. I however, trod in the footsteps of the thousands of Welsh emigrants before me who travelled on the 'boat train' from Pembroke, via Llanelli, (which teachers had told us was the largest town in the largest county in Wales), to Paddington Station, having sent my one small trunk of belongings ahead of me. Paddington Station is probably the most familiar London railway station for all South Walians and as my working-class roots had not provided access to the literary delights of Paddington Bear, it was to me simply the gateway to the rest of the world (which it might also have been for the duffle coated, bear, although I wouldn't know, having still not read any of the books). I have a huge nostalgia (or hiraeth as we Welsh call it) for Brunel's station, with its wonderful, glazed roof supported by magnificent iron arches. This nostalgia was both created and is fuelled by an unusual memory which embraces all of my senses: I often have a verbatim memory of conversations, particularly when they are linked with strong emotional experiences; I have a pronounced sense of smell which is also linked to memories, and music has the ability to transport me back through time and conjure up memories which have lain dormant for many years. I have memories from when I was very young; even before I could speak properly, which I had assumed everyone had and still find it difficult to believe that this is not the case. This memory of mine is both a blessing and a curse, as it enables me to reconnect with good times and experiences almost at will, but it can also play back memories of unhappy, unpleasant experiences and conversations when I least want them. These intrusive, visual and verbal 'flash-backs' can be difficult to deal with and as I have a tendency to ruminate, are also difficult for me to get rid of. I think though that they are balanced, or perhaps even outweighed by the pleasure of being able to experience joyous and happy memories, sometimes unexpectedly but also as a matter of choice. One of my favourite memories which I can conjure up and experience on demand, is of travelling 'home' from London, unaware at the time that Paddington Station would be filled with victorious Welsh rugby supporters who had just beaten the English at Twickenham. As was my usual habit, I arrived at the station breathless, only just in time to catch my train and I was met with the barrage of Welsh voices (mainly male) singing Sosban Fach (the anthem of my hometown) and Bread of Heaven, in a natural harmony as only the Welsh can. The sound of their singing reverberating around the glazed arched roofs of the station was such a powerful experience for me that it is no exaggeration to say it touched my heart and physically hurt. It moved me to tears and almost brought me to my knees, there on the dirty, oily platform, suffused by railway station smells. This memory remains to this day to be one of my most powerful and vivid ones, which I can still hear and feel whenever the need takes my fancy. The often misquoted verse written in a poem called 'In Passing' by Brian Harris written in 1967, just a few years before this says:

> *To be born in Wales,*
> *Not with a silver spoon in your mouth,*
> *But, with music in your blood*
> *And with poetry in your soul,*
> *Is a privilege indeed.*

and that privilege is most often seen in the almost physical need or compulsion that the Welsh have to either 'wax lyrical', or to raise their voices together in harmony at every opportunity or on any occasion. The sound of Welsh voices singing is always able to touch deep in my heart and soul and this experience in Paddington Station had the effect of elevating this architectural monument of Victorian industry to an almost church like status, or a place of pilgrimage for me. I now rarely go to London, choosing to avoid if it at all possible, and living in Sheffield means that my occasional visits take me through St Pancras: a railway station which although grand, will unfortunately never hold the same place in my heart.

My escape was prefaced by two or three years of anguish and despair which I internalised and didn't communicate to anyone, not even my long-term boyfriend. This may have been because I couldn't find the words to express what I was experiencing but with forty-eight years of hindsight, I now realise that it was more likely that I was unable to recognise, acknowledge, or articulate my feelings at that time as I had no idea what those feelings were or why I might be feeling the way I did. I had passed the 11 plus exam and attended an all-girls grammar school, much to my mother's relief as I had always said that I would have preferred to go to the secondary modern school, but I always had a sense of imposter syndrome and felt that I shouldn't really be there. I had always been a tom-boy who didn't get on with girls as I just didn't understand the girly stuff, and still don't. Outside of school, I had a great all male (except for me) friendship group where I was accepted as one of 'the gang'. We did exciting things together. I wasn't allowed a bike, but the boys lent me theirs and taught me to ride in an empty car park. They looked after me when we played endlessly on the local riverbank and in derelict garages. In school, I didn't fit in well in an all-girls environment and I only had one friend at a time to relate to. During lunch time, she and I used to sit on a grassy bank which formed the boundary between the Grammar School and the nearby Secondary Modern School's playing fields, where we chatted with two of the boys who I knew out of school. Despite being bright I only just got by academically and I realise now that I lacked the academic skills and motivation to achieve as I knew I could. I think that now, someone might recognise that I had weak executive functioning skills, but this was simply unheard of at the time, and I suspect that I was just labelled as 'disorganised', 'untidy' and 'lazy'. In fairness, I think that I was very skilled in devising ways to hide or mask my difficulties. Homework was a contradiction between the words home and work and to this day I don't know how I was allowed to get away without doing any. I do remember sometimes hurriedly scribbling something in panic, just before the teacher arrived in class, so that I at least had something to hand in, but I was never questioned about its many absences. My parents didn't seem to have any expectation that I should do schoolwork at home, so they never asked if I was doing any or what marks I was getting. Needless to say, I did badly in those subjects which required additional reading, or memorising rules or learning vocabulary, relying purely on my short-term memory and understanding of concepts, which was just about good enough for me to succeed, up to my GCEs. I walked the one and a half miles to and from school every day carrying a heavy, hand-made, leather satchel which contained my books for the whole of the week, because I realised this would enable me to just pick it up every morning with no preparation. I never knew which lessons I had on which day and in those days, with the exception of specialist subjects such as cookery or science, most lessons were delivered in the form room, so I didn't have to worry about being in the right place at the right time. I followed the other girls when we had to move classes, so it was never obvious that I didn't know where I was going, and my lack of organisation skills wasn't a problem as I had all I needed for the week in my satchel. If I hadn't brought ingredients for cooking, then I would just skip that lesson, and no one seemed to notice. The satchel had been made by a saddler in Llanelli market, according to my mother's rigid sense of what was traditionally required for a grammar school pupil. Unlike a rucksack, which I would probably have preferred, it had one long strap fastening in a buckle about three quarters of the way along. I shortened this by making an additional hole with a hammer and a nail, which enabled me to carry the heavy weight of weekly books high up on my back, on my left shoulder. This was never a problem for me, although I do now suffer with stiffness and rotator cuff injuries in that shoulder.

It seemed to me that the Grammar School focused only on pupils who wanted to go to university or teacher's training college and as I didn't aspire to either of these, I attracted no interest or attention whatsoever. The almost magical experience of having the one teacher who recognises your potential and takes an interest in you which then inspires you and changes your life, did not happen to me and it remains a mythical concept which I mourn. I still wonder what difference (if any) a special teacher might have made to the rest of my life. In short: despite doing well in my 'O' Levels I failed my 'A' Levels. I studied Zoology and Botany because there was no option of Biology, which I had excelled at and really wanted to study. Both 'Zoo and Bot' involved dissecting, drawing and memorising many classification lists. There was also 'homework' which as I've already mentioned was an anathema to me. I enjoyed the practical dissection lessons and had enough artistic ability to draw well enough, but the rest of the work, particularly the classification lists passed me by. As sixth formers we were given the privilege of using the prep rooms for private study, and Botany students could also use the greenhouse. I hated the prep room which was full of the posh, studious, girly girls and I didn't know how to study, so I never frequented it. My one friend, (who also wanted to study Biology) and I took the alternative option and spent our time between lessons chatting in the greenhouse, where it was warm and smelt of peat and geraniums, (more correctly called Pelargoniums). I loved this place, and the smell of geraniums is still a powerful positive memory for me. Linda, (my friend) quickly realised that Zoo and Bot bore no resemblance to the Biology which she and I wanted to study so she left to study nursing in Frenchey Hospital in Bristol. I have no idea why I didn't do something similar except that I think that I was unaware of the extent of my unhappiness and also had no awareness of other available options. I didn't want to be a nurse or a teacher, or an office worker, all of which I could have done with the 'O' Levels that I had, but I didn't know what other alternatives there might be. In retrospect, I recognise that I was bereft and isolated when Linda left, and I was lonely and at a loss without her. Neither of us made any effort to keep in touch which I now think was a bit odd as I thought we were close and still do. She introduced me to horse riding which I loved, and which partly fulfilled a childhood passion, but I didn't continue with this after she left, and I often wonder what happened to her. My attendance plummeted in direct correlation to the increase of my unhappiness; I did no work for two years and slept most of the time that I was in school and no one even noticed, or if they did, they didn't say or do anything. For some silly reason which I still don't quite understand, I insisted on sitting the exams despite not having done any work: I had no intention of attempting to answer any questions and wrote my name on the papers and then slept through the whole of the exam period. My sense of failure was enormous, and I drew the only conclusion that I could from this, which was that I wasn't very intelligent. My boyfriend had already left home for the bright lights of London, in Woolwich Polytechnic; I had no other friend, and I was lonely and miserable. My self-esteem was at rock bottom and the constant criticism, restrictions and controls that formed the basis of my home life didn't help either.

Moving to London was either sheer luck or coincidence, or if you are person of faith as am I, it was an answer to prayer. My parents, especially my mother, never really wanted me to leave home and the only option which they could accept was for me to follow in my sister's footsteps to the nearest teacher's training college which would enable me to either travel daily or return home every weekend.

That would have been very wrong for me on a number of levels, so I rejected it, cementing the already given reputation of a rebel and in the process making leaving home an impossibility for me. In retrospect I realise that I was very low emotionally and probably depressed at this time. I knew what I didn't want but I had no sense of what I could do, and I think that my father whose abilities and aspirations had been restricted by the unfairness and disadvantages of his life recognised this, as well as my need to stretch my wings, and when all seemed hopeless, he helped me find an acceptable way out.

My father had a highly developed social conscience and a strong sense of justice with left wing political beliefs, all of which, by this time were embedded in a practical Christian faith. He was fortunate to find an expression for all of this in the Salvation Army. I am very like him in many ways and all of my life have been passionate about social justice and equality with them both being a central expression of my faith. When I was younger, my father had befriended a man whose large family was living in extreme poverty due to periods of unemployment and imprisonment. His wife had resorted to prostitution to meet some of the family's needs and the family increased in number every time her husband was in prison. The husband treated every child as his own, but they were all very neglected and malnourished, living in obvious and extreme poverty. One of the younger children who was about two or three years younger than

I was particularly damaged by the family's lifestyle and was found by the courts to be extremely malnourished, vulnerable and unmanageable, so she was taken into the care of Social Services. She was placed in a local children's home and wasn't allowed contact with her family, so my father offered our home as a safe place for her to visit at weekends. Angela (as she was called) was certainly no Angel: she was feral as well as malnourished, with a fighting spirit and physical skills to match which made her a scary force to be reckoned with. I have never been easily frightened by people or things and perhaps, although I didn't realise it at the time, this was the reason why Angela took to me, and she and I got on famously. I seemed to understand her and she for some inexplicable reason seemed to idolise me and would do anything for me. She, like me, loved my father and we were friendly for a number of years. She moved away but appeared to have some sort of extra sensory radar so that she always turned up at my parents' every time I was visiting, and we were able to introduce our daughters to each other on a couple of occasions. I now think that Angela was probably autistic, but back then, Angela was just Angela: a feral, 'rough diamond' who wasn't able to communicate her needs in conventional ways and remained a force to be reckoned with.

Whatever label I might want, or not want to give to Angela, she inadvertently provided my introduction to the world of what was then Child Care Services and was the driving force behind a growing desire in me to become a Social Worker, or more specifically at that time, a Child Care Officer. Coincidentally in 1972, my father saw an advert in one of the Salvation Army magazines for Residential Child Care Officers in their residential homes all over the country and he encouraged me to apply for a position. This was to be my salvation and to my absolute joy, I was accepted for a position which could have been anywhere in the country but was at Avalon, a senior girls' approved school run by the Salvation Army in Chislehurst in Kent. This was a Godsend in more ways than one: I didn't know it then, but time would show that I had a particular talent for working with teenagers; in addition, Chislehurst was ironically only about 7 miles away from Woolwich, where my boyfriend was. There could not have been a more perfect opportunity for me to break free. Of course, my parents would never have approved of me moving to be so close to my boyfriend if it hadn't involved working in a residential position for the Salvation Army, but unknown to them, my great escape had begun.

It was perhaps a little naïve of me to think that escaping to work in a Girls Approved School, especially one run by the Salvation Army, would bring freedom and it didn't take long for me to discover that I had exchanged one prison for another, albeit a bit more of an 'open' one, which was also extremely beautiful. Chislehurst is almost the perfect English village with caves, duck ponds, a golf course and two small commons. It is also of historic interest as Napoleon III and his family lived in exile there for most of the 1870s. Being just 36 minutes from Charing Cross on the train, it is a commuter's dream. Coming from a council house in an industrial Welsh town, I thought it was very posh indeed and I would probably still think this as Chislehurst is indeed a very desirable and expensive London suburb. Avalon was (and I believe still is) a beautiful mansion house, built in 1872 nestling in leafy secluded elegance high up above one of the main roads between Bromley and Blackheath. I was awestruck by its size, beauty and opulence but soon discovered that I would have little time for appreciating this or exploring the delights that Chislehurst had to offer as the Approved School regime was brutal and exhausting: not just for the girls who were placed there, but also for the staff.

1972 was the last year in the life of Approved Schools, which were part of the criminal justice system, as the implementation of The Children's and Young Person's Act 1969 replaced them in 1973 with Community Homes with Education which came under the auspices of the local authority, as opposed to the courts. I'm told that this made little difference to how these institutions operated but the change of focus was at least a step in the right direction in terms of the treatment of those young people placed in them. As a Senior Girls Approved School, Avalon housed up to 27 young women between the ages of fifteen and eighteen. When I was there, one of the girls was pregnant.

All had been placed by the courts, generally for committing an offence which, if they had been an adult, would have resulted in imprisonment, or they had been found to be in need of care and protection and control which was most usually evidenced by: poor behaviour when on probation; or by persistent running away from Local Authority care, or activities such as theft or prostitution. The 1970s was a very sexually liberating time and issues such as coercive control or grooming were not recognised then, with a preference to viewing the victim, as an active and willing participator, and sometimes the perpetrator of their own abuse, despite their young age. I realise now that this had been the experiences of many of the girl who were at Avalon. I remember Georgia who had fallen madly in love with an older man when she was just fourteen, who had allowed him to tattoo his name, very badly across her back when she was so drunk that she didn't know what was happening to her. It was clear that he was controlling and abusing her but she so longed to be loved and wanted that she was totally unable to recognise this and was desperate to complete her 'sentence' to get back to him. She believed it when he told her that the tattoo served as a permanent reminder of his love for her, whilst in reality it was a constant and permanent reminder of his 'ownership' and control over her. Then there was Rosemary, a very pretty, child-like fifteen-year-old who was a real 'innocent' who seemed devoid of all emotions and who I thought was as bright as a button but who was said to have some sort of learning difficulty. She took everything at face value and accepted everything that she was told without question. She fell in with the wrong crowd of older boys and thought that they were her friends when in reality they took advantage of her. She naively did what they told her to do even when that involved stealing, shop lifting and having sex with multiple friends of theirs, to fund their habits. She remained fiercely loyal to them, refusing to name them, even when she was caught shoplifting and taken to court. I didn't think that she was unintelligent, but she was emotionally and socially naïve. There was also Marion who in my mind was an older, version of Angela. She was unrelentingly and fiercely independent and resisted being controlled but was intentionally and actively compliant in order to secure her leaving date as soon as possible. She also seemed to be able to distance herself from the reality of her situation. I made the mistake of thinking that I could arrange to visit her when she moved to a Dickensian type hostel in Hackney, but my visit resulted in her giving me the cold shoulder from an upstairs window which overlooked the street entrance. This experience shocked me as I was astounded that her Social Worker would move her from a place of opulence to a hostel in what was then such a filthy and run-down area. I often wonder what happened to her afterwards.

As well as being a stunning building, Avalon was also beautifully furnished and was managed by a woman who had aesthetically good taste and exacting standards of cleanliness and presentation which she promoted in all aspects of daily living. The manager was a budgeting wizard par excellence, and she did not compromise on the quality of furnishings so that Avalon was as perfect inside as outside. It was indeed a joy to behold. This Welsh working class, girl who had been born and brought up in a council house was starstruck, but quickly found out that this image of perfection came at a cost and was maintained by the hard physical work of the resident young women and the small team of four staff, including me. I had been brought up to work hard and I wasn't shy of physical work, but I found the regime at Avalon to be gruelling and exhausting. I was expected to work a six-day week, starting at either 6 or 7 am depending on whether I was on the rota for cooking breakfast and waking staff up with cups of tea or not. I was also on the rota for providing a 'motivational' talk for the day, at the end of breakfast. After the motivational talk, girls and staff would follow an extensive cleaning routine which staff would continue after the girls went into school. I sometimes had a couple of hours to myself in the afternoon when the girls were in their classes, when I would usually collapse and try to catch up on sleep, and I would then work until 10 30 pm, after which I would once again fall exhausted into bed. On my one day off a week, I had to return before the door was locked at 10 30 pm as we were not entrusted with a key. I learned what afternoon tea was and how to clear crumbs from the table with a Victorian silver-plated dustpan and brush which was designed for that purpose; how to cook on a huge industrial size coal fired Aga (which has put me off this form of cooking appliance for life); how to scrub and polish floors by hand; how to make beds with perfect envelope corners and I also acquired a new vocabulary which included words like 'ablutions' and 'absconded'. In the evenings, I would be required to sit at the back in the television room where every individual chair was placed strategically so that each girl could be observed to ensure that there were no interactions between them. I hated these aspects of the work although working alongside of the girls on cleaning tasks provided the only opportunity for meaningful one-to-one conversations with them, but despite loving these limited interactions, I found complying with the restrictions and the work regime exhausting. I felt like I was slowly losing the will to live, and I needed more sleep than was possible.

There was also the all-female thing again: try as I might, I just don't find it easy to get on with women and here I was again, immersed in an environment oozing with female hormones. At least there were three male teachers at school, whereas at Avalon, there, there were no men at all. I don't know what it is, but I just don't experience female bonding in the way I see other women do, certainly not in groups, and I get on much better with men. I don't think of this as a failure, but I do see it as an absence of something which I think I should have and would like to have at least some of the time;

perhaps because I see that other women appear to get a closeness and pleasure from it, but the fact remains that any pleasure eludes me. I do have an intense love and bonding with my two daughters which I didn't really experience with my own mother, but I don't see a causal link with this.

I had never experienced bullying before and I have personally been accused at times of being intimidating, but there was one, very unhappy, middle aged member of the staff team at Avalon who disliked me and picked on me regularly. I have already hinted that I have some sensory differences, and I am particularly sensitive (perhaps hyper-sensitive) to non-verbal communication and how it conveys emotions. This sensitivity can be crippling for me at times as I can pick up too much on other's feelings and then ruminate over them, but this woman oozed hostility without particularly having to do anything intentionally. It quickly became obvious that I was unable to do anything that would please her or be seen as right in her eyes. I'm usually quite strong emotionally but on this occasion, my physical exhaustion left little energy for emotional control, and I broke down in tears one morning in the middle of delivering my post breakfast 'motivational' talk. I was mortified but supported by the other staff who understood what was happening and how I felt. I don't know how the situation was managed but the negative 'vibes' stopped after that and I have never been bullied since.

I am forever grateful to the Salvation Army for giving me this opportunity as despite not knowing it at the time, it provided me with my second introduction to autism. With my 2020 knowledge, I can now recognise that some of the girls, including Georgia and Rosemary were probably autistic. For some inexplicable reason I was always drawn to them, and I was able to communicate effectively with them despite the restrictions of the punitive environment. I've often wondered why this was and realise now that this was linked to my relationship with my mother, which will be explored in later chapters.

Working at Avalon challenged my faith during which time I recognised that I had a 'holier than though' attitude towards practical Christianity. This manifested itself in a tendency to easily judge others for their failings, and I became wrongfully critical of the Salvation Army because of this. Over the years, the maturing of my faith and a better understanding of grace has altered this, and I am both repentant and grateful to the Salvation Army for its influence in my life. I'm also especially grateful to the Salvation Army for funding me at this time to take a City and Guilds course in Residential Child Care, which I did on a day release basis at what was then Southwark Further Education College. As I didn't have 'A' Levels, I needed this to gain a place on the Residential Social Work course at what was then the Polytechnic of North London and is now the University of North London. The one day a week course was a welcome relief from the daily domestic grind, and it opened my eyes to others' experiences of residential work, which were not as restrictive or as punitive as my own. I found that I could manage the academic work to pass the course easily, and I was accepted for the social work course at the Polytechnic of North London. They say that fortune favours the brave and my acceptance on the course was on condition of me gaining more experience by changing my job and I thanked God for this next stage of my escape.

My second job in Tower Hamlet's Assessment and Reception Centre couldn't have been more of a contrast. It was another large building but this time a former Victorian workhouse facing straight onto East India Dock Road, one of the most heavily trafficked roads in London. It was noisy and rough (as were the kids) and no amount of effort could keep it clean of the dirt from the traffic pollution which entered the building through every nook and cranny. My father, who visited both Avalon and Langley House, as it was called, couldn't understand why I had given up what he saw as the luxury of Avalon for the dirt and roughness of the east end. The kids were a challenge but fantastic, with some of the most horrific life stories, similar to Angela's and worse, but real east end 'rough diamonds', again, similar to Angela. It was a real education: I increased my vocabulary again but this time with very different types of words to ablutions and absconding; I learned how to break into my room when I had mistakenly left my key inside it, amongst other unmentionable things; I was free to experience the 'sex and drugs and rock and roll' of the 1970s, and apart from the drugs, I loved it. There was a large staff team who I tended to be on the periphery of and I was teased for my Welshness, but I once again had one friend, a mixed-race Londoner, who taught me everything I needed to know to survive. I had my freedom; I could come and go as I wanted, and no-one could keep me away from my boyfriend who was still in Woolwich. Langley House was the first place that really made me aware of autism, although I still didn't know the word at that time.

I very clearly remember a young Maltese man called Raymond. He was about fifteen, tall and physically mature. Raymond thankfully didn't stay with us for long as it was not a suitable environment for him. He had no spoken language and I was to recognise later that he was classically autistic. His parents had him late in life and his mother had recently died and his father, who obviously loved him very much, wasn't able to cope. Raymond found the lack of structure at Langley House very difficult and sought comfort in handling his penis most of the time and I remember the Senior House Mother, my team manager, causing him huge distress by teasing him, saying that she would 'cut it off'. I wish that I was the person then that I am now and that I knew then what I know now. I knew that her actions were wrong, and I did challenge her at the time as I could see that poor Raymond was taking her comments literally and was terrified. I was young and inexperienced whilst she was my manager and unlike me, was qualified, so my voice carried no weight. This is one memory from this time that I would rather not have as I can still visualise poor Raymond's face when she taunted him. Fortunately, Raymond only stayed with us for a few weeks until he returned to the care of his father.

I worked for six months at Langley House and then was allowed to continue to live there when I studied at the North London Polytechnic, travelling from East India Dock Road in Poplar to Highbury Grove in North London, every day from September 1973 to August 1974. I still lacked the academic skills to achieve as well as I thought I should, but I found that I could write well enough to get a high grade. The course was challenging in many ways, but it particularly challenged me to 'find myself'. This was the time that the Beatles involvement with the Maharishi Yogi had triggered an interest in Transcendental Meditation and along with smoking cannabis, this had spread into academic circles. 'Finding oneself' was not as much of a cliché as it is now and counselling as a taught subject was very much in its infancy. My personal tutor, Ernie, was a humanist and was very influenced by the American psychologist Carl Rogers. Ernie ran his tutorial group as an encounter group with the idea that we would learn about ourselves and how we operated in a group through interacting with each other, with no real structure or guidance from him as a facilitator. I found this very difficult as I never really knew what to expect or whether I was behaving appropriately or not. I did however learn a lot about group behaviour and dynamics, which was invaluable and which I still use in my everyday life, as well as at work. Ernie was a lovely man and in a one-to-one tutorial with me he asked me a question which I couldn't answer, and which haunted my thoughts for many years. The question simply was: 'who are you?' and I had absolutely no idea. I have only recently found the answer and I wish that Ernie was still around for me to tell him. I would now say:

I am a child of God

I am a woman

I am a wife

I am a mother

I am a grandmother

and I am a friend

I am an autism specialist practitioner

I am many things to many people

But most of all, I am me and I am content with that.

CHAPTER 2

Before me there was my mother

It has to be said that my mother, Gwyneth, was an unusual woman whom I would describe as a bit of a Jekyll and Hyde character. Family research suggests that she came from generations of long-lived, strong, resilient Welsh women who survived against the odds. Today, some might refer to her mother Martha, as a 'bloody difficult woman', but my memory of my grandmother is that she was physically tough and strong; a woman who spoke her mind and was emotionally resilient; fierce in her defence of the truth and those who she loved, and extremely capable in all circumstances. A woman, who I thought, could do anything and whom I idolised. My mother however, seemingly defied this genealogical heritage and was known throughout her life for her shyness, faddiness, and emotional frailty, as well as her absolute refusal to speak Welsh.

Both my grandparents were bi-lingual, with Welsh being the language of the home, or 'yr iaith yr aelwyd', as my grandmother would say. My mother, despite being able to understand everything that was addressed to her in Welsh, flatly refused to speak a word of it, and this continued throughout her life. Not only did she refuse to speak Welsh, but she was stubbornly and rudely resistant to any attempts by Welsh first language speakers who tried to communicate with her through that medium, often causing them huge offense. My father who was also bi-lingual used to tease her (in English and Welsh), saying that he used to have a dog who could understand Welsh but couldn't speak it, but my mother, despite being well known for her emotional volatility and argumentativeness, didn't on these occasions rise to the taunt. Later in life she always claimed that she 'didn't have a sense of humour' and I realise now that she saw my father's teasing as accurate, literal, matter of fact comments, so never felt the need to respond to them. I always thought that my mother's refusal to speak Welsh was because she was a perfectionist who couldn't bear others hearing any of the errors she might make. Similarly, she wouldn't allow others to hear her read, despite being able to read well, and I thought this was also because she was afraid of making mistakes. On reflection, later in life, I realised that she didn't like to hear the sound of her own voice, and also had some language difficulties: she often struggled for words and misused and mispronounced many English words, causing huge merriment in the family with her malapropisms. I wondered if she had a speech and language difficulty, particularly in the areas of semantics and pragmatics, and I suspect that she probably did have. I know now though that her inability, or what was perceived as an unwillingness to speak Welsh, is called receptive, or passive bilingualism.

Everyone in the small Welsh community that my mother was born into and brought up in knew that she was a bit 'odd' and everyone either accommodated or accepted her unusual behaviours, with a 'that's just Gwyneth' comment, or no comment at all. Whilst she was blissfully protected by this acceptance, her oddity wasn't completely ignored, and as an adult, stories of her habits and behaviours during her childhood and youth were often reiterated in an amusing but loving way. These stories describe a child who was always prone to emotional meltdowns and who always had to have her own way: her school was close to my grandmother's cottage, and it was well known that she would run home to her mother's protection at the first sign of any pressure from teachers. My grandmother was reportedly so fierce in her defence of her daughter that the teachers very quickly learned to 'tread on eggshells' around my mother, avoiding making demands of her. She was also inordinately fussy about food, in a household where everyone ate what was put in front of them without question. Stories were told of how the cream from the top of the milk had to be skimmed off and put on one side for her as she wouldn't drink anything else and also how she was fed chocolate as a substitute food. I never understood how this was allowed to happen, thinking that she would surely have eaten what she was given if she was hungry, but I was told that wasn't the case and that she would prefer to starve, rather than eat food she didn't like. I now understand how difficult it is to raise a child who doesn't eat well and how grateful parents are when they do eat something, but it always seemed unfair that my mother did not extend the same privilege to either me or my sister when we were growing up. I am still slightly surprised that my no fuss grandmother was so indulgent with my mother but realise now that she probably had no choice if she was to see her daughter thrive. I'm grateful though for these stories and anecdotes, as they provide an insight into my mother which I would not otherwise have and together with my retrospective analysis of my own experience, memories and events, enabled me at the age of fifty-one, to eventually realise that my mother wasn't just the most difficult woman on God's earth, but she was, of course, autistic.

My memories of my maternal grandmother are that she was a formidable woman who had strong views and was outspoken with them. She was also a matter of fact, down to earth woman who could do anything that she put her mind to, from making the lightest pastry and mouth-watering roast dinners with onion gravy, to building walls and clearing out blocked drains. She was a wonderful role model who had skills as a 'healer' with natural remedies for all common illnesses, garnered from pre-NHS days. As late as the 1950s she would be the person who would often be called on to help deliver babies and to lay people out when they died. Birth and death were part of life in her household, and she was matter of fact about both.

I didn't know my grandfather as he died when my mother was fifteen, but my father, who worked with him in the tin plate works, always told me that he was a very quiet, tolerant and patient man. I pictured a kindly man, dominated by the women of the household, subjected to what my father teasingly called 'petticoat government', but more recently have come to think that he was a gentle man, who didn't have much energy for family life because he worked long hours in a physically hard and demanding job. Both my grandparents worked in the Llanelli Tin-Plate and Stamping Works and my understanding is that this was where they met, although I find it difficult to see how love might have blossomed in such a harsh working environment. I've recently discovered that my grandfather had another side to his character: I was always puzzled as to why an old pump organ dominated the front room of my grandmother's tiny two up two down cottage, particularly as no one could play it. It stood idle, for about fifteen years after my grandfather's death, and later served as an interesting plaything for me and my sister in our early childhood, when we could pump pedals, pull out stops, and play strange eerie noises on it. I had no idea why it was there, but I've recently discovered that my grandfather came from a gifted musical family and he and his brother played the organ. I assume that this musicality was a gift as the family would not have been able to pay for music lessons. If it was, then it skipped a generation as my mother was one of the rare Welsh women who couldn't or wouldn't sing. Both my sister and I were musical, although I hated practicing the piano as I couldn't tolerate making mistakes and wanted immediate perfection, but I could sight sing almost anything, and singing remains one of my greatest pleasures.

My grandmother was thirty-five when she married, in a period when twenty-four was the average age for a woman. I was always told that the reason for both of my grandparents being older than most couples at the time was because my grandmother (Martha) had responsibilities for looking after her aging and sick parents. My grandmother had a reputation for being a woman of her word and there was a story told in the family that she made a 'deathbed promise' to her mother, to look after Sarah-Jane, who was her mother's ward, who possibly had some sort of learning difficulty which she herself always referred to as 'rheumatic on the nerves'. The continued keeping of this promise was a condition of her marriage to my grandfather and was maintained throughout their marriage, with Sarah-Jane becoming my grandmother's life-long companion until my grandmother's death in 1964. The continuation of the promise was then taken up by my parents, when Sara-Jane, known affectionately to everyone in the community as Auntie Jenny, and thought of by me and my sister as our third grandmother, was looked after by my parents until she died in 1975.

I also remember my grandmother telling me that she wanted no fuss when she got married. This was partly because of her nature and partly because she was an older bride with an even older groom so the wedding was planned for 8.30 am on a Sunday morning, thinking that this would provide some modicum of secrecy. She worshiped regularly at The Salvation Army, and had done for some years, but her marriage took place at the chapel which her in-laws attended and her soon to be brother-in-law was the organist. This surprises me as I know how loyal she was to the Salvation Army, and I would have expected her to stick rigidly to her own place of worship. I wonder if the reason for this may have been because the Salvation Army in Llanelli wasn't registered to conduct marriages at that time but as yet have no evidence for this. Whatever the reason, my compliant grandfather (Tom) agreed to the early start to satisfy his bride's desire for secrecy. Their efforts were thwarted however as they were so highly thought of in their community that the chapel was full to bursting, despite the early hour. I have doubted the accuracy of this as at the time of their marriage, Calfaria Chapel could seat seven hundred and eighty people, but my grandmother was known for her truthfulness. Recent research of Llanelli's history also confirms that Llanelli's numerous Chapels were always full on Sundays during this period. Whatever the accuracy of the story, it become a family legend and my mother, Gwyneth, was born just ten months later in the tiny, terraced cottage that had been in my grandmother's family for generations.

My mother was born on the 3rd August 1928 after a prolonged three-day labour, and throughout her life, was keen to emphatically correct anyone who suggested that she weighed a stone, as her recorded birth weight fell just one ounce short of that, at thirteen pounds fifteen ounces. Whilst surviving pictures show that she wasn't an overweight child, she suffered with obesity as an adult and was a self-confessed fussy or a faddy eater throughout her entire life.

People who knew my mother as a child and young adult described her as being 'spoilt' by the adults in her family. As I've already mentioned, she always had to have her own way with everything, as she firmly believed that any other way was the wrong way. This was a trait which continued throughout her life, and she had little or no control over her emotions if her will was thwarted. Others have described her as being 'frightened of her own shadow', 'a wall flower', being sheltered and needing protecting from everyone other than immediate family. School, as mentioned was particularly difficult for her and she remembered hiding for much of the time, refusing to take part in any activities, especially reading aloud. She hated being touched or getting dirty; used dolls as ornaments; was prone to inexplicable tantrums, would run home if a teacher as much as spoke to her, and took food fads to an extreme level. Her 'taste and trace' skills, enhanced by an acute sense of smell, were so sophisticated that she could track any hidden unliked or unwanted food item from a great distance and she could not be fooled by any food substitute. This incidentally was something that my mother never grew out of and throughout her life, she was heard to repeat the phrases 'I'm a fussy eater, see' and 'I'm a chocaholic', somewhat proudly, with shocking regularity. She was not good at communicating verbally and had a relatively limited vocabulary continuing to use children's vocabulary into adulthood. 'Ach a fi', (a Welsh statement of disgust) was a very common phrase which she used as a child and also throughout her life, only because she didn't realise that it was Welsh not English, and this was always used in relation to taste. She would describe even mild spicy food as 'burny' but craved strong peppermints and eucalyptus sweets and was insensitive to other types of pain. Rationing during the war was extremely difficult for her and her family members as her main foods were chocolate, double cream, and bread with thickly spread Welsh butter. Major meltdowns occurred if these foods weren't available, and no alternatives were acceptable to her. Her meltdowns were so great that other family members would sacrifice their rations for these foods to ensure that she was fed, but she showed no appreciation for this. The stories told were that this was particularly true of butter, which had to be Welsh and which she spread on bread 'with a trowel', for the whole of her life, refusing to tolerate any form of margarine.

I don't know much about my mother's teenage years: she left school at fourteen with no qualifications other than being able to bake Maids of Honour and her father died when she was fifteen. With no academic qualifications, the options open to her were either physical work in the tin plate works or shop work. My ever-protective grandmother recognised from her own experience that my mother's 'fragile emotional nature' would not survive the rigours and banter of the women's work in the tin-plate works and fought hard to secure her a position in the haberdashery department of a small family run department store in the town centre. It seems that she managed in this supportive environment and did well. She was particularly praised for her eye for colour, as she could match threads to fabric far better than others and could also spot discrepancies in patterns. She was proud of the nickname 'Hawkeye' which she earned there and which my father also used to describe her. She told me that she was different to the other shop girls, particularly in her sense of dress and refusal to wear any make up, which again was a lifelong habit. She had a hatred of lipstick as she said it was made from beetle's blood, which of course is true of the colouring cochineal, but she also claimed that it drained women's blood because their lips looked so pale when they removed it. She also didn't like the 'feel of it' on her lips, so she never wore it. She occasionally used face powder, but again preferred not to as she didn't like the smell of it.

By the time she was seventeen, my mother was tall, at five foot eight inches, slim and still very blonde. She remained shy and virginal, and men found her both intriguing and desirable. I was always told that she could have had her pick of any of the eligible young men in her community, but they had to first of all get past the protection of her somewhat formidable mother. She worked in the haberdashery department of the small department store for five and a half days a week, and any social life she might have had centred around the Salvation Army where she attended three times on a Sunday. My mother kept meticulous records which show that she met my father on the 30th September 1945 and her life changed forever.

I have chosen to use the word 'seemingly' with regard to my mother defying her heritage, as her shyness, faddiness, and emotional frailty was for outside of the home only and behind closed doors she too could have well been described as 'a bloody difficult woman'. She was totally unreasonable in her determination to rule the roost with a harridian iron fist. She was also able to hold a grudge and stubbornly maintain a silence well beyond the limits of what most people would consider possible. My father adored her, even though he claimed that she made his life miserable most of the time. As already mentioned, there was only ever two ways of doing things: Gwyneth's way and the wrong way. In the early years of their marriage, my father who was very much an alpha male would attempt to exert some influence and battle with her for control, but he never succeeded. He was never violent towards her, but my mother could be violent when provoked beyond her emotional capacity and control. I do remember that as I child I thought that they would separate, and I worried about who I would live with if they did, as I did not want to live with my mother. My mother showed little reasoning ability or negotiation skills, but my father realised that if he wanted their marriage to succeed then he would have to do things her way and submit to her mostly unreasonable demands. This was difficult for him as his natural inclination was to be in control. He also loved my mother and was proud to say that 'his word was his bond'. He was determined to keep his marriage vows and after a number of years this led him to the conclusion that outward subservience was the only solution to a stable family life. Volatile may perhaps be the most accurate word to describe our family life, as rows and arguments formed the basis of most, if not all of our communication and interactions. I have struggled over the years to recognise and to admit that ours was a dysfunctional family, but I believe that others might consider it so.

I loved my mother and try to portray her favourably, but the truth is that she was a control freak who was very prone to emotional outbursts. Any inability to control a situation or individual resulted in rage and sometimes physical violence. Alternatively, she would resort to long periods of weeping and wailing which could last for days or even weeks. These were exhausting for all of us and we all 'walked on eggshells' in our attempts to prevent and avoid them. Her approach to parenting was that babies and small children were to be managed and controlled. Childcare in general was likened to a series of military manoeuvres which had to be battled with and overcome and she worked her way relentlessly through the required tasks, leaving my father to provide the emotional component. Teenage years were difficult as previously compliant children became 'rebellious' and control was challenged, and I dealt with this by leaving home as soon as I was able to.

Unknown to me at this time, my mother was, of course my first introduction to autism. She was also probably the biggest influence in the development of my lifelong interest and passion for autism which led to my subsequent career in this field. She first taught me how to listen, understand and communicate with autistic people: a lesson for which I am eternally grateful.

Autism was unheard of in the 1930s, but I would hope that in 2021, a child who presented similar non-typical development and behaviours as my mother would be identified as being possibly autistic and would be referred for diagnostic assessment. Unfortunately, the most up to date figures from the National Autistic Society suggest otherwise with the most recent estimates still demonstrating a 3:1 male to female ratio.

Diagnoses of adult women also suggest that many girls are still not being diagnosed in childhood. There are a number of suggestions which are put forward to explain this including that:

- autism is an expression of an extreme male brain or an extreme form of maleness so that the prevalence of autism in males is therefore likely to be higher.
- the higher ratio in of autistic males might be linked to genetic or biological factors such as testosterone or chromosomes.
- the female presentation of autism is subtly different to the male and as the diagnostic criteria and tools are based on the male presentation, there is a bias towards a higher male diagnosis
- women and girls are better than their male peers at covering up or 'masking' any social or communication difficulties that they may experience. This leads to professionals (especially teachers who are at the frontline in identification for diagnoses), failing to identify and initiate the diagnostic process.

My personal view, based on my now long experience of supporting both autistic males and females, and other gender identities not mentioned in the research, is inclined towards the last two explanations. These figures and explanations are however to a certain extent irrelevant given that autism was unheard of early in my mother's life. It wasn't however until 2004, after I had been working with autistic people for approximately thirty years, that I recognised that my mother was not just a very difficult woman, but was in fact autistic, and if assessed even at that late stage in her life, would probably have been given the label of Asperger Syndrome.

I still wonder why it took me so long to recognise this.

This revelation (which is explored in detail in Chapter 7 of this book) was 'better late than never' as it was a positive turning point in what had previously been a difficult and challenging relationship. The change this revelation brought about in my understanding of my mother and my subsequent ability to relate differently to her from the time of realisation onwards, caused me considerable regret for the lost years, and I often wondered how I could possibly have missed what in retrospect were obvious indicators of autism. I was reminded of the Biblical quote that *'God would restore the years that the hungry locusts had eaten'* and these were both a comfort and a truth for me during the latter years of my mother's life. A truth for which I am eternally grateful.

It came as somewhat of a relief to hear that I was not alone as an Autism specialist practitioner, in failing to recognise autism in someone close to me, as even Tony Attwood had a similar experience with not recognising that his son had Asperger Syndrome for the first thirty-five years of his life. It does seem that it's sometimes difficult for some of us to see the obvious when that person is so close to us, and emotions and family relationships and familiarity cloud our perceptions.

My revelation was not of the road to Damascus type but rather one of a slow drip feed. I had been brought up in a close, narrow minded, Welsh community, but within that my family was particularly insular and, in many ways, secretive. I am still reluctant to use the word 'dysfunctional' as it brings shame, and my family did function albeit in a non-typical way, but I have to acknowledge that my family was, as described very volatile. Interpersonal relationships were not healthy, being grounded in arguments and confrontation and the powerful nature and impact of words wasn't recognised or understood. The negative words used have had a life-time's impact and effect on me and my self-image: personal insults were hurled at one another, and compliments were absent. No one visited us or was allowed over the threshold, and we rarely visited other families. I grew up thinking that this was true of all families and that arguments were a healthy form of communication. When I moved to England in 1972, I identified differences in other people's life experiences but attributed my family experience to Welsh, working class stereotypes as portrayed in media representation of the time. When I was welcomed into my husband's family in 1981, I saw how an emotionally healthy family functioned, and made a conscious decision to learn from it and raise my children differently to how I had been raised, but for some inexplicable reason I still stuck rigidly to my explanation of typical Welsh working-class family life. This perception remained until I was asked to act as independent autism advocate for an autistic man who coincidently lived in Llanelli, just a few streets away from my parents. Working with him caused me to identify similarities with my mother and helped me to identify that what I was seeing was autism and not working class Welshness. I began to see at the age of fifty that my family wasn't typically Welsh, but was different to most other Welsh families, and that my mother was indeed autistic.

An apology to my mother

If you were here now, I would tell you that I'm sorry.
Sorry that I didn't know
Sorry that I got it wrong for so long
Sorry that I should have seen and didn't
Sorry that I misunderstood.

If you were here now, I would tell you that I understand.
I understand your anxiety and your compulsions
I understand your fears
I understand that you're different
And that's OK.

If you were here now, I would buy you a kaleidoscope
And look at colours with you
I would ask you questions and listen to your answers
I would learn more about you and wouldn't argue
I would tell you that I love you.
If only you were here now.

CHAPTER 3

It takes two to tango

As well as my mother there was my father: he was a complex man who was born in 1925, at least one generation too soon, into what can only be described as poverty. He was the second of four children, born to parents who were also first cousins. This relationship both intrigues and confuses me. Despite their mothers being sisters, my grandmother and grandfather seem to have had quite different social upbringings and experiences; one in North and the other in South Wales. My grandfather was described as 'rough and ready'; a 'man's man' from industrial South Wales, who enjoyed rugby, beer, fighting and women. His occupation, according to the 1911 census. was a builder's labourer. My grandmother on the other hand, as I knew her, was a 'bit of a lady' who was from North Wales. She was born in the slate quarry area of Blaenau-Ffestiniog, and her father was a quarry man, but she was brought up for most of her early life in a little terrace house facing onto the beautiful and picturesque sandy cove of Borth-y-Gest, in Gwynedd, where the family moved to when she

was about two years old. Borth-y-Gest is now an attractive
and desirable holiday location, and it seems that its
potential for this, dates from the mid nineteenth century,
when it was mainly known as a centre for ship building.
Whilst both of her older brothers became mariners, her
father remained a quarry man until his death in 1907,
at which time my grandmother was nine years old. The
story told in the family was that her mother survived and
supported the family by taking in lodgers until she then
married a baker three years later. The latter part of this
is confirmed by census and marriage records, but for
me, the intriguing part of the unsolved puzzle is how my
grandmother, Esther, who was the daughter of a quarry
man and the stepdaughter of a baker, became 'a bit of a
lady', who learnt to play the piano and was sufficiently
well educated when the family relocated to Liverpool,
to become a secretary to the manager of the Graysons
Shipping Company. I'm also intrigued as to how and why
this prim, proper, professional woman who came from
North Wales but lived in Liverpool as an adult, married
her 'rough and ready' first cousin who lived in Llanelli in
South Wales.

Historically, marriages between cousins in the United
Kingdom were not uncommon, particularly amongst the
upper classes, as the practice ensured that wealth and
property remained in the same family for generations.
The limited physical mobility of the time also had the
effect of narrowing the pool of marriageable young men

and women to those contacts within the family circle. The expansion of the railways in the late nineteenth century changed this however and provided opportunities further afield for increasing wealth and employment, as well as providing increased access to eligible spouses. Queen Victoria, the great matriarchal example and role model for the country's women, married her first cousin, prince Albert, and it was well known that this alliance resulted in the passing on of the recessive genetic disorder Haemophilia to their children. Perhaps this, together with the growth of scientific enquiry by such scientists as Charles Darwin who himself married his first cousin, led to the post Victorian concern in the increase of recessive genetic conditions in the children of what were termed consanguineous marriages. Whatever the reason, by the late nineteenth century interest in inherited congenital conditions was rife and first cousin marriages were increasingly being questioned. Scientific studies at the time failed to prove conclusively that there was an increased risk of autosomal recessive conditions in first cousin marriages but despite this, first cousin marriages very quickly became frowned upon. By the early twentieth century such marriages, although not illegal had become unusual. My father, being born in 1925 to parents who were first cousins, was subjected to social stigmatisation and prejudice for much of his childhood because of this, and this stigma, together with his younger brother having a form of congenital deafness, was something that concerned him well into his adult life, prompting him to conduct his own research into the subject. He recalled that the stigma was so great that one of his grandmothers hated him, precisely for this reason.

Other stories that my father told also indicate that he was a bit of a feral child who took great pleasure in playing tricks on people and who loved being naughty. One example from his early schooling was that he was sent to his headmaster to account for a misdemeanour and was about to be caned but avoided the punishment by kicking the headmaster in his shins and running home. Needless to say, this resulted in a quick change of schools which the school records show as happening during his first year at school, when he was aged five. He had a lifelong interest in and a love of all animals and told how he used to make pets of mice which shared the occupancy of the riverside slum housing in which the family lived. Even in his eighties, he would chuckle and relish in retelling the story of the havoc that he caused by throwing one of these mice onto his grandmother's aproned lap. I have no doubt that this will have been only one of such incidents as he was forever rescuing hedgehogs and damaged birds when I was a child, so I have always suspected that his grandmother's apparent dislike of him related more to his feral, rebellious nature and his love of being 'naughty' (as well as her dislike for mice), than it did to his consanguineous heritage. He however was adamant that he was correct in his understanding of the basis of her negative feelings and prejudice towards him and I can only assume that she must have given him cause to think that this was true.

From what I understand and observed, the rebellious, feral boy grew up to be a rebellious, intelligent, self-educated man who continued to love being 'naughty' and 'winding people up' throughout his life but who also, perhaps because of his personal experience of stigma and prejudice had a strong sense of fairness, equality and justice which he directed in defence of the underdog. Alongside of his rebellious, challenging streak, he had what seemed to me the contradictory traits of a rigid liking for order, rules and regulations, coupled with a strong sense of correctness, duty and responsibility.

He loved arguing, critiquing, and debating and had a passion for left wing politics but his real love was for all things legal. If he had been born at a different time or into a different social class, he would have followed a career in Law, but this was not an opportunity available to the poor, self-educated young man who started his life in slum housing. Later in his life he would find satisfaction in channelling this passion through trade union activities where he successfully represented and advocated for many of his colleagues who had been unfairly treated by their employer, often doing this in an official capacity at tribunals.

I know little about my father's childhood and youth but suspect that school did not feature highly or regularly in it. He was literate and numerate but had huge gaps in his general knowledge and education, accompanied by an advanced scholarly knowledge in self-taught areas of passion and interest. He talked often of being poor as a child and he broke my heart when he told me that he grew up thinking that he must have been very naughty because Father Christmas never came to him. The often-quoted adult statement to children that Father Christmas would only visit them if they were good, had been accepted, quite literally by him and his experience and logic was that as Father Christmas didn't visit him, he must have been very naughty. He always said that he was well fed, and loved what I considered to be the monotonous, regularly repeated weekly dinner menu which my grandmother was very skilled in providing from a limited and restrictive household budget, but he also told stories about his father drunkenly stealing chickens to make sure that they had one for their Christmas dinner. He also talked about being coached by his mother, in providing persuasive 'sob stories' to shop keepers when clothes and shoes needed to be replaced and there was insufficient money to pay for them: something which my grandmother would vehemently and embarrassedly deny in her old age. I believe that the gaps in his education occurred because the bulk of his learning was gained from working on building sites with his father, which is where he preferred to be.

My father grew up quickly, and like his father before him, was also a very physical, 'man's man'. He had enormous hands which were hardened by the hard, physical graft of labouring alongside his father from a young age, and he loved adventure and excitement. The outbreak of the Second World War in 1939 was exciting to him and at the age of fourteen he was propelled out of whatever school there might have been, into the adult world of the local tin plate works where he replaced an eighteen-year-old man who had been called up to military service. It was here that without knowing it that he worked alongside his future wife's father. He found being immersed in the 'man's world' exciting at first but became bored with the daily grind. He joined the Local Defence Volunteers and became an Air Raid Warden and soon thought that the life of a soldier would be more glamorous, thrilling and financially more lucrative. As a young adult, he had film star good looks, and was (like his father), a heavy drinker (drinking ten pints most nights), and a fighter. He was fearless, claiming throughout his life to never having experienced fear. He also had a strong sense of national pride for Wales and wanted to defend his hometown, which was being targeted by the Luftwaffe because of its industrial contribution to the war effort. He craved more excitement and was so keen to enlist and join the fighting ranks that at seventeen he cheated his age to sign up and, in his words, 'take the King's shilling'. At this time, he was the oldest of my grandmother's three surviving children, her first child, a daughter, having died of septicaemia following a tooth extraction, at the age of six. I cannot imagine how she, or my grandfather who had served in the First World War and knew the sort of horrors that soldiers would experience, reacted to this but I was always told that he was fearless and unstoppable in his fixed, perhaps rigid determination to seek excitement and adventure and see more of the world, as well as 'doing his bit' for his country.

What I know of my father's army career is 'interesting': he had, throughout his life, this curious mix of loving law, order, duty and routine whilst also being rebellious and challenging, and what I know of his military service reflected this. Like most army veterans who served on the front line, he didn't talk about his experience of the war. I did learn that he drunk a lot; was reprimanded for fighting when drunk; was wounded; struck up a relationship with a well-endowed Belgian woman called Maria, (with photographs to prove it); went AWOL and was hidden by the said Maria (who I have always referred to as 'the lovely Maria with the big boobies',) and also was promoted from Private, to Corporal, then in 1946, to Sergeant when stationed in a Prisoner of War Camp in Berkshire. It was only many years later when he talked to my husband about the horrors of the D-Day landings, and we took him and my mother on a trip to Normandy that I learned about the horrendous events that he had witnessed and taken part in whilst liberating France from the Germans. I still find it difficult to reconcile this fearless, fighting machine of a man with the father who I knew and loved.

My mother and father were in many ways the most unlikely match imaginable: she was a shy, innocent, naive seventeen-year-old who had been shielded throughout her life by a protective mother and he was a man who had grown up before his time and had seen the world. Their getting together was one of life's great coincidences and the survival of their marriage for over sixty years defies all expectations and explanation. It is both a mystery and a testament to my father's devotion, perseverance, and loyalty, as well as a product of the times.

Whilst my father was a feral, rebel child who became this superbly fit, fighting machine of a man, his younger brother was a very much smaller, sickly, frail child who was plagued by ill health throughout his life: the apple of his mother's eye. This sickly, frail brother embraced Welsh non-conformism with a passion, which was to lead to him later in life becoming a circuit preacher of the old school. It seems that in 1945 the chapels in Llanelli were also one of the few places where respectable young people could mingle and meet, under the cover of the Cymanfa Ganu, which might be described to the non-Welsh as religious 'sing a longs'. My father's brother was one of the young men who was 'doing the rounds' of the Cymanfa Ganu at this time, looking for a respectable young woman to 'walk out' with. Whilst the Salvation Army was not part of this Welsh tradition, it was, and still is known for its musical tradition and this drew many eligible young men in search of suitable young women to its meetings.

Also at this time, following the German surrender in 1945, my father, was stationed at a prisoner of war camp in

Berkshire. He was also, like his brother, passionate in his beliefs but unlike his brother was embracing communism and atheism.

My mother loved keeping lists and records of dates and events which were important to her, so thanks to the survival of these, I know that she met my father on the 30th September 1945. My father loved telling and retelling the story of how they met, primarily because it was a tale of love at first sight but more importantly for him, was a tale of how he quite literally swept her off her feet. The story he told was that on the night of the 30th September 1945, he was home on leave and he was at a bit of a loose end as Llanelli, being in Carmarthenshire, was 'dry' on a Sunday so he was unable to go to the pub for his usual ten pints. His younger brother was going to a meeting in the Salvation Army because there was a visiting brass band, and he suggested that my father went with him, not for a moment expecting that my father, the almost confirmed atheist would accept. For some odd reason, or perhaps because he had some ulterior motive, my father did go with him. My mother was just seventeen years old, and was tall and blonde, sitting with the Songsters (choir) on the raised platform in the Citadel. My father spotted her immediately and thought that she was the most attractive woman there. He asked his brother who she was and was told "that's Gwyneth" to which he replied, 'I'm taking her home tonight'. This caused his brother to laugh because he knew that a friend of his had already arranged to take my mother home. My father had no recollection of the next one and a half or two hours of the meeting, or the quality of the band or sermon, because he only had eyes for my mother. As the meeting reached its conclusion, and whilst the last prayer was being said, he was 'on the starting blocks' and quickly went to the front of the hall, and took my mother by the arm saying, "I'm Des and I'm taking you home tonight". She went with him, leaving his brother and his friends with their mouths agape. My father loved telling this story and laughed at his audacity for the rest of his life.

My father also loved writing simple poetry and every Valentine's Day throughout their sixty-one years of marriage, bar the one when they weren't on speaking terms, he would write a simple poem for my mother. One Valentine's Day after they had been married for forty something years, he put his memory of their meeting in writing, and I am fortunate enough to have the original of this and be able to copy it here. He would love to know that he has eventually had something that he had written published and I'm sure that he would once again chuckle as he read it.

The poem:

Gwyneth
Do you remember that distant day
I came to hear that brass band play
I sat and wondered who you were
And my heart began to stir

Tall and blonde with a lovely smile
I kept watching all the while
What's her name I asked a boy
And he replied with tones of joy

That's Gwyneth – she's my date
I thought my lad you are too late
She's taken my fancy and this I know
Tonight with me she's gonna go

I walked you home with step so light
I saw you again the following night
Crafty old cupid had fired his bow
My heart was pierced I loved you so.

Forty years and a couple more
I've lain at your side – heard you snore
Joys and tears ups and downs
Laughs and smiles and scowls and frowns
I've loved you more with passing time
Rain hail snow and shine
Because you are my Valentine.

And the rest as they say, is history.

CHAPTER 4

The early years

History, or at least stories, coupled with my mother's notes and sentimental keepsakes, show that after the fateful meeting in the Salvation Army on 30th of September 1945, my parents conducted a distanced, but romantic relationship. My father went back to working in the Prisoner of War camp and my mother continued living with my grandmother and working in the department store. They wrote to each other, sending photographs with little pencilled notes, one of which is included in the photographs, and my father sent short amusing poems expressing his love for her. He proposed to her and sent his mother money with instructions for her to take my mother to a jeweller for them to buy a ring of my mother's choosing. The budget wasn't discussed, and my mother lacked the communication skills to ask my grandmother how much my father had sent. My grandmother, being always thrifty, kept quiet and my mother chose a ring which she liked but was inferior to one which she aspired to. Unknown to her at the time my father's budget of

£35.00 would have been sufficient for her to have the 'ring of her dreams' but this didn't happen. They announced their engagement on the 3rd September 1946, but my mother who could hold a grudge better than anyone, harboured a resentment to my thrifty grandmother for the rest of her life, for her inferior ring. She insisted that it was replaced for their silver wedding anniversary, when my father bought her the three stone diamond ring which was a version of the ring which she had originally coveted.

My father was discharged from active service on the 10th June 1947 and like every other soldier, he was given a demobilisation grant and a set of civilian clothing, which included a "demob suit", a couple of shirts, underwear, a raincoat, a hat and a pair of shoes. He also had glowing testimonials from his commanding officer and the German prisoner of war officers. He married my mother in the Salvation Army Citadel at 10 am on the 28th August 1948 and they honeymooned for a week in Bournemouth. My mother had never left her hometown, so it was a pivotal moment for her and a life experience which led to Bournemouth being the only holiday destination which was acceptable to my mother, throughout her life. My sister was conceived in Bournemouth and was always referred to as a 'honeymoon baby' as a result.

My mother had strong views, which I would term an obsession against premarital sex, and this haunted her throughout her pregnancy, as she was terrified that her baby would be born early, so people would think that she was already pregnant when she got married. She repeatedly told me how a cousin of hers who 'had to get married' was continually suggesting that this was also the case for her, and how this had caused a long-held rift between them. To her immense relief, my sister was born in my grandmother's house, at 2.45 am, on Thursday the 16th June 1949, weighing nine pounds, with the date ensuring that my mother's reputation remained intact. I have to often remind myself that this was 1949 and that my mother, who had experienced a very narrow upbringing was still only twenty at this time and that many young women were concerned to provide proof of their virginity. My mother's hatred of premarital sex was extreme however and it became a life-long fixation, which was to be the source of many family difficulties in later years.

So: one plus one made three!

My mother had little imagination. She had a doll as a child who she had named Anne, after a deceased relative and she had always said that she would also call her child Anne. My father joked with her about what name they would give to a boy, but she was unable to contemplate having a boy as a realistic possibility. When fortunately blessed with a baby girl, she reputedly asked my father what they would call her, to which he replied: 'Anne of course'. I like to think that he said this out of love for his wife and a desire to please her, but the reality was that he knew that the choice of name was non-negotiable.

So: Anne it was. Apparently, my father was besotted with his baby daughter: he often repeated a story of how he and my mother were travelling on a bus to visit a relative, with the baby in his arms, and his expression was such that the bus conductress commented that the baby was 'all his own work'. His pride in that was evident every time he told the story and on reflection, I think this provided the seeds for what was to become a never-ending competition between my mother and my sister for my father's affections. A competition which was heavily weighted in my mother's favour and in which she was victorious. My mother on the other hand thought that having a baby was just the same as having a doll who she could dress up and show off. Unfortunately, her baby didn't sleep, refused the breast, and cried most of the time so she was quickly disillusioned. I was always told that my grandmother, Auntie Jenny and my mother took it in turns 'walking the floorboards' every night and day with a crying baby, for many months, as my father was working shifts in the steel works and needed to be able to sleep. My mother was prone to oversharing and empathy also wasn't one of either of my parents' most obvious traits, so my sister and I were repeatedly told that Anne had always been a difficult baby. My mother often related a story of how Anne 'always wanted the moon as a child', but never in a positive or humorous way as it was always followed with the comment 'and still does'. This story's roots came from when Anne was about eighteen months old and was being taken in her pram on a moonlit evening to visit my father's mother, whose house was at the top of the highest hill in the town and afforded wonderful views. Anne was captivated by the full moon in the sky and reached out to it, repeatedly demanding that she wanted it. My parents found this amusing at the time, but their inability to provide Anne with the desired moon resulted in a major and lengthy tantrum. I think this is quite a charming story but the retelling of it as an illustration of Anne being a difficult baby and child, with the added negative comment, continued into adulthood and I do wonder about the emotional effect that this may have had on her. This will have been exacerbated by my mother making comparisons with me, when I was born, reiterating that I was 'such a good baby' that she and my father 'thought that they had a doll'. Whilst I wasn't responsible, nor did I ask for this praise or comparison with my sister, it did please me as a young child and it was only as an adult that I began to realise the potentially damaging effects which it might have had on my sister and her relationship with me.

My observations of my mother with other people's babies and then later, with her grandchildren confirmed my long-held belief that she approached motherhood as a military battle which had to be won at all costs. She prided herself in being able to get babies off to sleep by binding them tightly in a blanket and 'fighting' with them, rocking them until they eventually surrendered to her will, and closed their eyes, and then she would comment proudly

on not having 'lost the knack'. My father encouraged her
to breast feed my sister and me, believing, long before the
slogan, that 'breast was best' but she disliked the thought
of this and was relieved when her first born 'refused the
breast' and preferred to be bottle fed. She also had an
aversion to nappy changing, hating the smell of both urine
and faeces, and being overly concerned that she might
soil her hands. She was able to indulge in her aversion as
my grandmother and Aunty Jenny (as well as my father)
would shield her from the task and undertake it whenever
needed. I'm told that her experience of my babyhood was
different as the additional caretakers weren't available
at that time. I was given physical care, but little overt
affection and I have wondered if a lifetime of gut related
health problems might be linked to the potty-training
regime which I experienced, but Anne benefited from the
affection lavished on her by my grandmother and Aunty
Jenny, as well as my father, which perhaps compensated
for what were seen as my mother's deficits. Their presence
and support also diffused or prevented the rages that my
mother experienced when her baby would not conform to
her expected and desired expectations and routines. My
mother always found it difficult to control or regulate her
emotions so was prone to emotional outbursts. My father
told me that on one occasion, during the Salvation Army
meeting, she observed that I was not behaving as she
expected for Aunty Jenny, who was tasked with looking
after me, and she marched down from the platform in

front of everyone, took me outside and 'shook me like a little rabbit'. My father however adored babies and toddlers and disapproved strongly of this style of parenting which was common in the 1950s. He would take great pleasure throughout his life in rocking and singing to babies and young children and all four of his grandchildren have fond memories of him singing his signature tune, 'You Are My Sunshine' to them. He protected us from my mother's impatience and frustrations and potential for violence and often diffused situations. I suspect he challenged my mother about this and that rows ensued, as their relationship was always extremely volatile and at this point, he hadn't yet realised that the survival of his marriage depended on his willingness to surrender to my mother's demands. He was a hard worker and a good provider and was earning good money in the steel works when my sister was born and as my grandmother expected no rent, my mother was able to indulge in dressing up her human doll in expensive new outfits to show her off, every Sunday. I was told that this was excessively obvious to everyone and that others in the Salvation Army would comment to her about it. This was another resentment that my mother added to her list and held for the rest of her life, often repeating one comment from one named woman in verbatim, well into my adulthood.

My father was very much an alpha male; a man's man who throughout his life opined regularly (somewhat tongue in cheek), about what he called 'petticoat government'. He also desired a home of his own and felt confined and restricted by the cramped living conditions of a female dominated one-and-a-half-up and two down terraced cottage. He was an influential campaigner and used his skills to lobby and apply for a newly built council house in what was known as 'the rural' which was an area on the outskirts of Llanelli. My mother was rigidly, and in some ways irrationally attached to the cottage that she was born in, where she, my father and sister slept and lived in one small room and which only had an outside tap and toilet, so she found the concept of moving away from my grandmother's house traumatic. She wasn't enticed by the newness of the council house and the distance of two miles seemed like the other side of the world to her, so she was fiercely resistant to the move. Miraculously, she was persuaded and somehow, after nearly four years of marriage and living with my grandmother and Aunty Jenny, my by then pregnant mother and father became the first tenants of a newly built council house in the rural district of Llanelli, which had the luxury of water heated by a back boiler, a modern 1950's kitchen and a bathroom with an inside toilet. This was just in time for their second baby (me) to be born a few months later.

This move may have been traumatic for my mother, but I believe that it was more traumatic for my sister who was left behind, living with my grandmother. I have hinted at my mother's fixations and rigidly obsessive interests and at this time her interest was focussed on a particular school. She was convinced that the school that she attended as a child, which was only four minutes' walk from my grandmother's house was the only suitable school for my sister and was fiercely unrelenting in her opposition to any suggestion that my sister should attend any other school. My sister was due to start school when she was four years' old, so my parents decided to leave her with my grandmother when they moved house, in order to secure her place in the school of my mother's choice. This must have been a double trauma for my three-and-a-half-year-old sister, who then had to deal with both the loss of her parents and then a short while afterwards the 'cuckoo in the nest'. I think this caused irreparable damage and provided the foundation for the life-long difficult sibling relationship of the future.

My recent research into the council housing estate where my parents moved to revealed that the estate was only partially built in 1952 with significant on-going building work and many roads still in need of surfacing. My mother who was very much a town girl was unhappy living in the 'rural' with my father at work all day, despite the comforts of a new modern home and she couldn't find a routine for herself. She had no housekeeping skills, couldn't cook and missed the routine and company that her previous life which her mother and Aunty Jenny provided. Her detailed log of my father's employment history only starts from 1955, but my birth certificate in 1952, records that he was still working as a Millman in the Sheet Mills, which was part of the local steel industry. This was hard physical labour, and it would have involved shift work, leaving my mother alone some nights. My mother found her new life lonely and isolating. She missed the female companionship and support of her mother's home, so she regularly walked the two miles to visit her mother until very late into her pregnancy.

Another rigid fixation of my mother's concerned alcohol, and she had an irrational fear of it, or perhaps more precisely those who drank it. My father still enjoyed a drink at this time and on one occasion he returned home from celebrating at a friend's wedding to find that he was locked out of the house and that my mother was once again in 'melt down'. I don't know how this was resolved but for the rest of my childhood and until he became a Salvationist, he only drank at home at Christmas and had little contact with his previous friends, as this was the only solution to pacify my mother's unreasonable reactions and demands. It may have been that this was the reported occasion that my mother 'left him', walking the two miles back to her mother who took the attitude that she had 'made her bed so had to lie in it', and immediately walked back with her, to our home. Perhaps their marriage, would not have survived, if my grandmother hadn't done this as their relationship continued to be intense, volatile and acrimonious. Despite this, they did seem to work through it.

And then we were three again!

I was born in this new house and family at 1.45 p.m. on the twelfth of December 1952, delivered by the same midwife (nurse Griffiths) who had delivered my sister three and a half years before. I was smaller than my sister, weighing eight pounds twelve ounces. My birth certificate records that Aunty Jenny was present at my birth and my mother's permanently held resentment records that my grandmother wasn't, as she had to leave my mother during her labour, in order to return to her home because my uncle (my mother's younger brother) was returning from National Service in Germany. I have never known anyone who could hold and remember a resentment for as long as my mother, and throughout her life, she told me repeatedly that my grandmother used the phrase 'my boy is coming home' as a reason for 'abandoning' her in her hour of need. That however had no impact on me and my only reference to my uncle's return was that he brought the most amazing German doll home for my sister, which she kept amongst her hoarded possessions until her death in 2013, and which I always envied.

Naming me was less straight forward as my mother had become fixated on a name which had been given to a distant family member, and she wanted to call me Aldyth. English people wrongly assume that Aldyth is a relatively common Welsh name, but it was (and probably still is) unknown in Wales. My father was opposed to me being called this and he unusually stood up to my mother over it. I was told that my father's refusal to call me Aldyth, resulted in me being called Christine as a compromise, because I was born close to Christmas. Unfortunately,

I was given Aldyth as a middle name and suffered teasing and embarrassment throughout my childhood and teenage years because of it.

I was repeatedly told throughout my life that my parents thought that they had been gifted with a doll when I was born, particularly when they compared me to my sister. I was apparently a calm and settled baby who slept when expected and fitted into my mother's rigid routines. My doll like qualities were added to as I grew a bit older as I was a 'pretty baby with a happy temperament and a winning smile'. My father continued with his belief in 'breast is best' and encouraged my mother with this and unlike my sister, I took to it. My mother continued to prefer bottle feeding but unusually chose to please my father and persevered for three months before introducing me to the bottle, (another thing that I perhaps unreasonably attribute to causing over forty years of chronic ulcerative colitis). On reflection, I think that my mother's isolation enabled her to bond with me in a way that she wasn't able to with my sister but her oversharing of her feelings and preference towards her second baby was yet another one of those seeds which when left to germinate contributed to the life-long difficult familial relationships. This was particularly so when put into the context of my sister remaining at my grandmother's house for the duration of this period. Whilst at a young age, I basked in the praise which I received for something which was not gained from any effort on my part, I realised the unfairness and the damage caused by this as I grew up. Unlike my sister who was a 'girly girl', I grew up to be a feisty tomboy, and despite being the younger, I defended my sister, physically and emotionally from attacks both outside and inside of the home, throughout our lives. In my adult life, my repeated mantra in my late-night discussions with my father was 'we are the product of our genes and our environment', and I think he did his best to understand this, but I still grieve for the close sibling relationship that I never had.

I know little of the two or so years that my parents lived in their new house, except that my father, who was a great homemaker loved his new home and the community that grew up on the estate. My mother however continued to be unhappy and longed to return to her roots. Her rigid perseverance, insistence and demands, again won out and my father's lobbying skills were once again utilised to secure a move to the house which was to become our permanent family home. This house was (and still is) precisely 176 yards from where my mother and sister were born and where my grandmother lived. My parents bought it from the council as part of Margaret Thatcher's Right to Buy policy, in the early 1980s and both of my parents were rigidly determined to live in this house forever, so it remained the family home for fifty-seven years until my mother died in 2011, just eighteen months after my father. All my childhood and teenage memories and experiences were formed in this house and are explored in following chapters.

My maternal grandmother circa 1910, wearing her Salvation Army bonnet.

My paternal grandmother. She was a bit of a lady.

My maternal grandparents' wedding photograph.

My only picture of my 'rough and ready' paternal grand-father. Taken in 1947 with my mother, my grandmother and my uncle.

My mother with her mother and Aunty Jenny in 1947, just after she met my father. Taken at my grandmother's cottage.

My mother aged 4, with her 'ornamental' doll called Anne.

My mother aged 5, looking anxious.

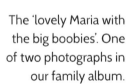

The 'lovely Maria with the big boobies'. One of two photographs in our family album.

My father (on the left), with his smouldering film star looks, and his friend. Sent to my mother shortly after their first meeting.

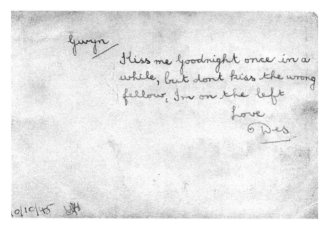

Gwyn

Kiss me goodnight once in a while, but don't kiss the wrong fellow, I'm on the left

Love
Des

10/10/45

My father's message to my mother, written on the back of the previous photo of him with his friend.

My parents' wedding photo.

Me at 13 months old.

An example of Owain's 'arty' pictures: it's me hanging from the branch of a tree.

Another example of one of Owain's photographs of me. He rejected this one because it's not very flattering of me. I've included it despite this because it shows my hair during its 'growing out' stage and I'm wearing the horse brasses pendant which Owain made for me as a present.

CHAPTER 5

The childhood years

I have already said that I have an 'unusual' memory and people tell me that I'm able to remember things from an earlier age than most other people. Memory is a wonderful thing, but memories can be mistakenly confused with pictures, stories, and other's recollections so that they sometimes require verifying to establish their authenticity. One such memory of mine which originally seemed so strange to me that it required confirmation from my mother was of me as a toddler, sitting on my mother's lap in a large van with an unknown driver whilst my mother pointed out a house to him. My mother confirmed that this memory was an accurate recollection from when I was eighteen months old, and we moved to a new house so that she could return to her roots and be closer to her mother and the home of her birth. I don't know if the move was traumatic for me, but I have a number of other memories from the same period: I remember the terraced house that we moved into being dark and gloomy with all of the woodwork painted a dark brown with the wallpaper being a lighter shade of the same colour; I have vivid visual and olfactory memories of wet wallpaper and I can visualise my father scraping it off the walls and also burning the paint off the woodwork. I clearly remember 'helping him' to scrape the paper off, with a little blunt knife that he considered safe for me to use, and I also remember wanting to scrape where he was scraping and not in the area that had been allocated to me. The smell of the brown paint melting under my father's blow torch is to this day, especially nostalgic for me and I also remember sitting on the stairs, watching the treacly melting paint running down from his shave hook whilst he burnt the paint on the bannister rail and allowed me to help by pumping the blow torch when it needed more pressure to feed the flame. I think this must have taken many weeks of work and it is a time of closeness with my father which I love to remember. I have always loved and been skilled at decorating and I suspect that this links back to these nostalgic times. I also remember my sister returning to live with us although I'm not certain if this was immediately after we moved in or if there was a time lag. Parenting was quite different in the 1950s, and children were given freedoms and independence which would be unthinkable now. We wouldn't now expect a five or six-year-old to walk home from school to her new home for the first time, unaccompanied, but this is what was expected of my sister. She had visited the house before but houses in a terrace look much the same to a five-year-old, and she walked up and down the street a number of times, looking for the right house, before my mother looked for her and found her. I clearly remember how upset she was when she was found and eventually came in: in hindsight, another mishandled situation for her. Our 'new' home was probably built in the late 1920s or early 30s but my architect husband has suggested that it was to a much older design and specification, with only a stone sink and a fireplace with a back boiler which heated the water, in the tiny kitchen which was known as a scullery. It had an outside toilet and coal house, but it did have a bathroom which only had a bath in it. The house backed onto a chapel cemetery with a narrow back lane in between, and my mother, very quickly realised that we were getting unwelcome visitors in the form of field mice who were in search of food and warmth. She disliked all animals intensely, finding them too furry, unpredictable and beyond her control, but immediately demanded a cat so another vivid memory of mine from this time was of two older women coming to the house with a little black and white kitten. My mother's imagination didn't extend to choosing names for pets. Dogs had to be called Chum, budgies had to be called Joey and cats were to be called Fluff, so our cat was Fluff. My mother maintained an intense dislike for Fluff who remained my cherished pet for nineteen years and we saw no more mice in the house for the rest of her life. She died of old age, shortly after I had left home. The house remained undecorated and uncarpeted for many years after my father had scraped the wallpaper and burnt all of the paint off and I find it difficult to understand why this was. My mother was never a homemaker, and she didn't seem to be aware of our lack of comfort or of our desire for a home which we could welcome people into, and she actively discouraged any visitors. She seemed to be content with just a roof over her head especially when that roof was only three minutes' walk away from her birth home and her mother.

My memories of childhood are of living in secret and shameful poverty and acknowledging this still creates feelings of guilt and shame. I don't think that a lack of income was the cause although my mother's records indicate that my father had short periods of unemployment between low-income jobs and also that he changed jobs relatively frequently, before finding his niche when I was twelve, as a meter reader for the South Wales Electricity Board; nor do I think that this was the experience of any of my contemporaries. I believe that whilst we would never have been well off, what I have called our 'secret poverty' was more related to my mother's inability to manage money, combined with her fixed and rigid fixation in only 'buying the best' (which she couldn't afford), and 'refusing the rest'. She was also unable to prioritise essentials and was unconsciously unreasonable in her fixation on quality and luxury items and shops. We had no washing machine because my mother was unable (or unwilling) to consider having a twin tub and automatic machines were well beyond our means; we had no carpets, because she could only consider the best quality wool carpets from the most expensive shop, which again, were unaffordable; she attempted to cook on what was called a Baby Belling cooker which only had a small oven and one small hot plate so when my father cooked Sunday dinner he had to put saucepans on the coal fire to boil; we had saucepans, but no cooking utensils so my mother used a knife for everything and I remember watching her in awe as she skilfully and successfully lifted eggs out of a frying pan, balancing them on the blade of a knife, and we also had insufficient bedding. My sister and I slept together in a double bed in a north facing room in a non-centrally heated house, and we were cold in the winter months. My mother's maternal skills didn't extend to night-time care, so we would wake my father and he would cover us with his heavy Army great coat. There was no change of sheets, and both my sister and I remembered that our feet tore the sheets when we stretched our legs out, because they were worn so thinly. I also remember my mother recycling the torn sheets as tea towels and dusters, but I don't think this was unusual for a 1950s housewife. This way of living was shameful, especially to my father and we grew up knowing that it was a secret which should remain indoors, so no one knew how we actually lived.

My mother was full of contradictions: she loved numbers and arithmetic and would enjoy making lists of shopping and costs, but a working concept of money eluded her, and she was incapable of budgeting, running a house and making it homely. She was obsessed by certain brands and fixated on certain items so that she insisted that my sister and I had a Silver Cross doll's pram each, which at the time of writing retail at £1,500.00, but we then wouldn't be allowed to play with them for fear of marking them. Christmas was a time of indulgence and extravagance, both of food and toys, which were bought from catalogues, and then paid for weekly, throughout the year. Expensive dolls were bought only for show, and we were only allowed to take them out for walks in our doll's prams to the local park, when accompanied, but they were not to be played with as we would spoil their hair or clothes. Our school uniforms were bought with Provident Cheques (a type of loan which incurred high interest and was then paid off for the rest of the year), from the limited stores which were part of the Provident Cheque scheme and the few other clothes we had were ordered from the same catalogue as the toys, and then paid off weekly. I once caused a major catastrophe when I was very young, because my love of rummaging through wardrobes unearthed some already wrapped small 'stocking filler' presents, which I of course unwrapped and unsuccessfully tried to rewrap, only for this to be discovered by 'Father Christmas' on Christmas Eve. My mother was distraught at this discovery, and it is only with many years of retrospective thinking that

I realise what mayhem I caused and why my mother had a meltdown of enormous proportions. Christmas Day was spoilt, and I remember being very confused by my mother's insistence that is was I who had spoilt it as I still enjoyed opening the badly rewrapped gifts. Food was bought from the corner shop, with my mother placing a weekly order with no consideration of the cost. She indulged in her food fads regardless of the expense but didn't or couldn't cook. Meals were peculiar to say the least: my father cooked Sunday dinner and eventually taught my mother how to do this, but bread and butter formed the basis of most of our other meals and was even eaten with tinned fruit and tinned rice pudding as a main meal. If certain vegetables were in season, then my mother would buy them so we would often have a plate of broad beans, fresh peas, or green beans, with butter and pepper, and nothing else, other than the obligatory bread and butter; or occasionally a plate of fried mushrooms, also accompanied by bread and butter. When I was eight, my father became a commercial traveller for three years and his travelling took him to the ports of Pembrokeshire where he was often given smoked haddock which he would bring home. My mother would boil this and then serve it on its own, once again with the compulsory bread and butter. We didn't complain as we didn't know that this was an odd way of eating or that it was any different to how others ate, and we also knew that any complaints would have the potential for triggering a dramatic scene.

My father, like many 1950s working class men, handed over his pay packet to his wife at the end of each week and received a small amount of pocket money in return. Because my mother was good with numbers and seemingly appeared to be managing, he trusted her and was unaware of the debts that she was accumulating. My mother had no friends, and she didn't welcome any of my father's friends, so no one came to visit. She would only answer the door to expected, routine callers such as the rent collector, and would hide from all other callers, so outwardly, everything seemed to be functioning well, and our hidden poverty remained our secret shame. Anyone who knew us would have been taken in by outward appearances and would have been shocked to see how we were actually living and the rest of us, especially my father, would have been mortified if our secret was revealed to anyone.

Alongside of this, my mother ruled with an iron hand from her own chair, which no one else would dare to sit in. She had no particular child rearing philosophy and I suspect that if asked, she would not have been familiar with the term 'corporal punishment' but in the absence of other adults to help her manage her children and her emotions, she kept what she called a 'Ginny Cane' in the corner at the side of her chair. This was a bamboo cane which she would threaten me and my sister with if she was unable to control our behaviour. My memory is that the threat of the Ginny Cane was greater than its use and I only remember being hit on the back of my legs with it once. It disappeared from the corner next to my mother's chair with no explanation and was then replaced with the threat of my father's leather belt, which as far as I recall was never used on us. I suspect that my father disapproved of the use of the cane, especially given his experience of being caned at school, and that he was instrumental in its removal from my mother's corner, but I'm not certain. My mother's hands however provided equally painful weapons which she frequently used when she couldn't manage her emotions, to inflict her punishments on us.

My sister and I had very different types of personalities and we dealt with my mother's violence and rages in different ways: I think that I, being more like my father, was the more overtly naughty child, but I was also funny, so I would either diffuse the potential situation with humour or I would out-wit and out-run my mother until her temper subsided in physical exhaustion. My sister, on the other hand found more devious ways to avoid potential trouble. We both avoided opportunities for punishment by playing outside most of the time and only returned home for meals which was quite typical for children of our generation. This seemed to suit my mother who was content to just issue warnings like: 'Don't play near the river or you'll get Polio', which always seemed rather odd to me as neither of us could swim, so a warning about drowning might have been more appropriate. Generally speaking, though, we were both acutely aware of how easy it was to trigger my mother's moods, so we 'walked on eggshells' around her most of the time, always being careful not to crack the fragile surface.

My overall memories of my childhood years were mixed. I have fond memories of playing in the garden with my sister and an older boy who lived two doors down from us. Like many children in the 1950s, we invented our own play: we would make walkie talkies from used tin cans and string, and trail them across the garden walls to speak to each other. These rarely worked, but it was fun pretending and I was always given the more daring task of walking along the top of the high wall to set the 'equipment' up which I greatly enjoyed. We would make mud pies and fill washing up bottles with water, to 'wage war' with a family of boys who lived on a street parallel to ours on the other side of the chapel cemetery and I was always tasked with the role of pedalling over on my tricycle to entice them to chase me back into our territory where we would pelt them with the ready-made mud pies and squirt them with water, all from the safety of our garden wall. I would also be directed to climb the wall into the cemetery to retrieve balls, whilst my sister kept watch and warned of the impending doom of the formidable 'Cem lady', who was the chapel caretaker who always wore a black beret, and who would box my ears if she caught me. Needless to say, she never did, as she was quite old, and I was very adept at sliding down the telegraph pole wire next to the wall, to escape her. We would also play on waste ground close by and make amazing dens in amongst the large plants which we mistakenly called 'wild rhubarb' but which I think may have been knotweed. This outside play also provided a wonderful escape from the tension and warring that existed within the home.

I am aware that I may have so far presented my father as a bit of a conundrum or a contradiction: I have described him as a strong, physical 'man's man', who had seen the world in the most heroic and horrendous of circumstances, but I've also described him as someone who readily gave in to his wife. My description so far has misrepresented my father as a man who was brow beaten by his wife which was never the case. My parents' relationship was always intense, confrontational, and volatile and was the source of considerable distress for me when I was growing up.

I idolised my father and was emotionally close to him when I was growing up. He was proud of me and liked the fact that I was a tomboy to the extent that he taught me to box and introduced me to his work mates as his son. As a feminist mother of two daughters, I am horrified at the sexism in this and I am aware that it could have had a negative effect on my identity, confidence and self-perception, but I am not aware of any conflict or difficulty caused by it, and at the time, I basked in what I saw as my father's compliment, without realising the effect that this could have had on my girly sister. I quite simply adored him. My mother's unpredictable changes of moods and extreme emotional outbursts on the other hand unsettled and scared me to the extent that I had the contradictory emotions of loving but not liking her and I found growing up in an environment that was characterised by verbally violent rows, confrontation and uncertainty, whilst my parents challenged each other for dominance and control, to be difficult and stressful. My father wrestled with reconciling his alpha maleness, with his love and loyalty for a woman who was confusingly domineering and controlling at home but who was also socially and emotionally dependent on him when outside. He had a rigid adherence to keeping his word and at times, his marriage vows were the only thing that kept him with my mother. He adored her but struggled to live with her and talked about leaving her throughout his life, but his love and sense of duty towards her remained passionate and strong. In retrospect I realise that he walked a thin line between loving my mother and protecting his children whilst at the same time maintaining his self-respect as a man, and also keeping faithful to his promises. It took many years before he realised that he had to be the one to relinquish control as my mother was immovable once she had fixated on something, but he never willingly surrendered to her demands, and this caused a fractiousness in the family that was difficult to live with. Similarly, he understood that my mother, by her own admission 'didn't have a sense of humour', but he never gave up on teasing and provoking her and he relished in the negative reaction which inevitably followed. My husband likened this to poking a sleeping bear to find out what its reaction would be: a situation in which the person poking the bear would always be aware that the reaction would be negative but was compelled to do it anyway. I'm not sure why he did this except that it seemed to be a compulsion: he enjoyed being naughty and perhaps had a misguided sense of fun mixed with a little empathy and awareness; he found it funny, even though he knew that my mother 'didn't have a sense of humour'. Whatever the reason, the impact on me as a child was that I lived in a constant state of anxiety for many years, whilst I anticipated their imminent separation and divorce. This came to a head when I was about nine or ten and my father left the house following a huge row with my mother, taking me with him. He took me to the cinema where we watched a Western and a supporting film before returning home a number of hours later. I remember enjoying the film and the precious time with him, but my memory is that it was tinged with anxiety as I worried about how my mother would receive us when we returned home. The reality was that there was no confrontation as my mother had already gone to bed, and life resumed with a silent frostiness. I however constantly worried that my parents would divorce. Whilst this would in many ways have been a relief, it caused high levels of anxiety as if given the choice I would have wanted to live with my father, but I was fully aware that in this situation, at this period in time, the decision would be taken from me and I would automatically have to live with my mother. This was something which I dreaded and continued to be something which I worried about throughout my childhood.

My mother's debts eventually caught up with her in about 1960, when the owner of the corner shop where she bought all of our food, presented her with a final demand for a number of unpaid, weekly grocery bills. This forced her to reveal the extent of her debts to my father and once again, there was a catastrophising drama, accompanied by weeping and wailing. Discussions took place in private so I'm not aware of their content, but the outcome was that my mother returned to work, in a local dress shop in May 1961. She wasn't able to adapt to the environment or relate to the manager but was fortunate after just six weeks to be able to return to the family run department store where she had worked prior to her marriage, and she continued to work there until it closed in 1969. In time, the debts were cleared, and she did finally get the Hoover Keymatic automatic washing machine that she coveted but our home wasn't decorated until many years later, after my father successfully persuaded her that I should be able to invite my teenage friends into our front room. She received a small redundancy payment from the department store and after 6 months found her niche working on the tills in the Co-op supermarket. An understanding manager excused her from shelf filling and allowed her to be the only member of the team who worked solely on the check-out, which she loved, and she remained working at the Co-op until her retirement in the late 1980s. Her experience of debt and her liking for numbers did however have a positive effect and as she learned how to balance her budget, she discovered a liking for saving. From this time onwards, the Christmas indulgencies were always covered by her 'Christmas savings bank' and there were no more financial worries, although it must be said that her savings took on a life of their own and became another fixation.

My mother was an excellent shop worker and she enjoyed returning to the familiar environment of her previous role, but she was only able to do and be one thing at a time and was unable to balance work with motherhood and running the home. My father stepped up and took responsibility for fire lighting on his return from work every day and cleaning the house on a Saturday; food was bought but cooking and meal planning was non-existent. I was sent to my grandmother's every morning before school for breakfast which was always a duck egg with toast, and my sister and I both had school dinners, but evening meals existed of tinned fruit, or tinned rice pudding, with the obligatory bread and butter and often cake. Aunty Jenny was given a key to our house, and she would visit every day to do some basic cleaning and tidying which my mother would have been unable to manage without. My recollection is that my concern for my father not having a hot meal prompted me to take on the role of family cook a year or two later. I always knew that this was in response to my mother starting work, but I thought that I was around twelve or thirteen at the time until my sister corrected my recollection of this, informing me that I was in fact younger. This would be confirmed by my mother's notes where she dates her return to work to when I was eight and a half which would then suggest that I will have started cooking for the family when I was about ten years' old. I enjoyed cooking and I'm told that I'm a good cook but cooking for the family in a way which met my mother's exacting expectations and timings was in itself quite challenging. Alongside of this I was expected to do well at school and attend weekly Salvation Army events such as meetings, choir and band practices. My mother was also fixated on my sister and me learning the piano. I realise now that this might have been because her father was a proficient organ player, but the piano was not the right instrument for me, and I didn't practice. I pleaded to give up but was not allowed to until I had successfully passed my Grade 5 exams, so this was added to my weekly 'to do list'.

My mother's fixation on our junior school was extended into a fixation on the Grammar School which required me and my sister passing the eleven plus exam which my sister successfully achieved in 1960. The Junior school which we both attended had two classes in each year group and passing the eleven plus was dependent on which teacher's class we were allocated to for our final year at school, with Mr David's class being viewed as being the almost automatic key to success. I knew that my mother had pinned all her hopes in me getting into Mr David's class, but I also knew that she was concerned that this might not happen. Her lack of confidence in me damaged my confidence in my ability, but my response was to adopt a bravado which manifested itself in a fake 'don't care' attitude and I openly stated that I didn't want to go the Grammar School which in my view was snobbish, and that I would much prefer to go to the local Secondary Modern School whose uniform I preferred. My mother despaired with me and on the day that I was told which teacher's class I would be moving in to, I thought it would be funny to repay her lack of confidence in me by playing a joke on her. Unlike my father, I had not realised at this time that my mother lacked a sense of humour. After school, I went to play at a friend's house, and I left a note on the dining table telling my parents where I was. I added a postscript to this note which said: 'by the way, I've been put in Miss Thomas's class'. Whilst this still makes me laugh, it had a catastrophic effect on my mother when she read it and it isn't an exaggeration to say that she became hysterical. My sister was immediately dispatched to collect me from my friend's house, whilst my mother wept and wailed to my father about how they would have to find money from somewhere to pay for me to have private tuition in order to ensure that I would then pass the eleven plus. I remember my sister's incredulity on the way home when I told her that it was all a joke and that I had been allocated to the higher echelons of Mr David's class. This was perhaps one of the shortest-lived meltdowns that I remember my mother having, as peace reigned once I confessed to it being a joke and she realised that I had in fact been successful. I genuinely thought this was funny and didn't realise at the time how devasting this would be for my mother. I now see echoes of my father's humour in this, and I recall that he, unlike my mother did see the funny side of my intended joke and I received no punishment. My mother's lack of confidence in me continued however but my much-loved grandmother had faith in me. She told me that she had half a crown put aside to give to me as a congratulatory present for passing the eleven plus. She unfortunately died on the day of the results in 1964 so never had her confidence in me confirmed, but I was still given the half a crown. I like to think that her confidence was unshakable and that she died knowing that I had been successful without the need for confirmation.

I, on the other hand continued to believe that I was better suited to the Secondary Modern School.

To my Grandmother
If you were here now
I would thank you for that half a crown and for the confidence you had in me
I would watch you cook and learn from you and share recipes with you
I would ask you questions about life
And treasure your answers

If you were here now
I would learn to speak Welsh with you
And sing hymns with you
I would go blackberry picking with you
And speak only the truth.

If you were here now
I would ask about Jenny
I would ask about herbs and remedies and write
them down.
I would tell you how strong you are
And that you are still loved.

If only you were here now.

CHAPTER 6

The teenage years

Donna Williams (aka Polly Samuel), writing in the foreword of Autism: An Inside-Out Approach describes her autism as having trouble with connections which then leads to her having trouble with tolerance and control. Both of my parents had issues with tolerance and control which now causes me to wonder if they may have also had problems with connections.

Later in her book Autism: An Inside-Out Approach Donna explains how problems in these three areas relate to the specific 'typical' diagnostic features of autism and she also lists some specific problems which autistic people may encounter in these three areas.

Under problems of Control, she lists:

- Compulsion
- Obsession
- Acute anxiety

Under Problems of Tolerance she lists:

- Sensory hypersensitivity
- Emotional hypersensitivity

Under problems of Connection she lists:

- Attention problems
- Perceptual problems
- Systems integration problems
- Left-right hemisphere problems

All of the above are related to how an individual responds to, copes with and makes sense of themselves and the world.

Donna Williams has been my autistic hero since first reading Autism: an Inside-Out Approach in 1996 and her work has underpinned the whole of my professional practice since then. I count myself privileged to have known her personally and to have been able to call her a friend, if only for a short time, and I continue to mourn her death and further contribution to our autistic knowledge and understanding. This inside-out thinking, and her subsequent work has influenced and directed the whole of my professional practice but unfortunately, I didn't know anything about any of this in 1972 and by this time, my need to escape my controlling parents had reached, as I described in Chapter 1, heights of desperation.

I was a teenager in the sixties and seventies, just at the end of the generation that thought that they had discovered sex and drugs and rock and roll: the 'flower power' or 'hippy' generation, (if flower power ever really reached South Wales). Whilst I was never really a hippy, I was greatly influenced by my artistic, eccentric boyfriend who was creative and adventurous in his sense of fashion. I am eternally grateful for this as I had little dress sense and as I spent Monday to Friday in school uniform and then Sundays in Salvation Army uniform, I had little chance to experiment or develop any. My boyfriend, Owain, who I had fallen in love with in 1966, when I was thirteen was 'unusual'; a swimmer and rugby player, as well as an intellectual; an 'eccentric', and an artist. I, like most 1960s teenagers loved the Beatles but he introduced me to the music of Bob Dylan, Jimi Hendrix, Joni Mitchell and Leonard Cohen as well as the books of Tolstoy and Zola. Whilst I loved Zola and enjoyed listening to records and singing along with the music, I was out of my depth with Tolstoy and didn't fit in, or certainly got very bored, with Owain's older, middleclass, intellectual friends, who would discuss the hidden 'real' meaning of Bob Dylan's lyrics, ad infinitum.

I met Owain because he was a school friend of some of the boys from the Salvation Army who I used to hang out with, affectionately known as 'the gang'. Until he came along, I was just 'one of the boys' but Owain brought a level of testosterone and sexuality to the group which wasn't there before. In retrospect, I think it may have been there, but I was completely unaware of it, probably because I was just on the cusp of puberty and still a tomboy. Owain was a year older than I was, he was tall, good looking in a 'different' sort of way, physical and competitive and he absolutely oozed a Mick Jagger type of sexuality. Teenage lust, mingled with oxytocin and testosterone, soon turned us into boyfriend and girlfriend: and a relationship which fortunately was to last for the next ten years developed. Oxytocin (the love hormone) did its work, and I was madly in love. As my family life was grounded in confrontation, accusations and control this relationship was bound to add fuel to what was already a toxic mix.

Strangely, my father reacted to it quite well: he liked Owain and didn't have many of the prejudices and fears that my mother had, particularly towards sex. My mother however was obsessed with sex but as with most things concerning my mother, this obsession was not straightforward, reasonable or logical. I rarely use the word 'obsessed' in relation to autistic people because of the negative connotations that it conveys, but I am unable to find a more accurate term for my mother's excessive interests in this particular area.

My mother had many fixed and rigid boundaries in her life, but they were mostly not typical of someone of her age and the time period, and somewhat confusingly in some areas, her boundaries were also noticeably absent.

This was particularly the case with bodily functions and sexual matters, where she was prone to, and unaware of 'over sharing': something which I thought was quite natural until relatively recently and also recognise that it's a trait which I also share. Because of this, sex wasn't a secret in our house, and I grew up knowing that my parents had a healthy sex life and that my mother enjoyed sex. I always knew that she was a virgin when she married my father and that my sister was conceived when they were on honeymoon. There was even a picture of the honeymoon bed in our family album, just to prove it! What puzzled me from the moment that I became aware of sexual relationships was why she insisted that my father who had 'seen the world' and who told stories of 'the lovely Maria with the big boobies' hiding him in Belgium for weeks when he was AWOL and living 'on the edge', was also a virgin when they met. My mother's intrenched belief did not come about from any deceit on my father's part and the photos that he had of Maria, which my mother (rather oddly) put in the family album clearly indicated an attachment and attraction to what was very obviously a sensual woman. Added to this, my father would also openly chuckle and indicate that he was not an innocent, every time that she made claim to his virginity. As an adult, I openly asked her if she genuinely believed that my father had not had sex before he met her, and she rigidly insisted on keeping to what could only be her fantasy of them both being pure and 'untouched'.

A visit to the D Day landings sites in Normandy in 2001 sparked my father's desire to visit Belgium and my husband and I took him and my mother on holiday to Bruges in 2003. Whilst there, we took the opportunity to take him to Ghent, where the 'lovely Maria' came from. When there, my husband and I greatly enjoyed teasing my father about the possibility of an elderly woman called Maria, being pushed in a wheelchair by a man in his sixties who looked suspiciously like him, accosting us in the street, weeping with joy that her lover (my father) had at last returned to her and their (now adult) son. My mother heard all this and smiled one of her fake smiles as the three of us giggled, but she still maintained her 'innocence' and insistence of her version of events. Her obsession with sex was in some ways linked to this, as she was quite literally obsessed, not with sex per se, but with the 'wrongness' of sex outside of marriage. This obsession dominated her life and had a major impact on mine and my sister's lives.

My mother's obsession, coupled with her need to control her teenage children and her lack of a concept of privacy, or the need for it, made our lives Hell. We quite simply had no privacy whatsoever: my underwear was examined for signs of sexual activity before being washed; gaps in curtains were peered through if Owain and I were alone in our front room, 'to see if there was anything going on'; she would not go to bed until I arrived home, however tired she was in order to 'see what sort of state I was in', and anything written would be found and scrutinised. I have never kept a diary despite loving to write, relying on my memory instead, and I suspect that fear of my mother's prying was the main reason for this. Owain would catch the last bus home from the top of our street, at 10 pm and I would be allowed to walk to the bus stop with him, but my mother frequently followed us to spy on us to make sure that there was nothing untoward going on. If I returned home later than she expected, she would not accept that the bus was late but would interrogate me, looking for some other reason behind the delay. There was one occasion when she came after us, when another boy from 'the gang' had come to the bus stop with us. Owain's bus was pulling off, and the other boy and I were just returning home, when she arrived, and for some reason, which I never understood, she flew into a rage, in the middle of what was a main road, and slapped my face, in front of this other boy. Whilst my mother often lashed out in her rages, the shock and humiliation of this particular outburst has stayed with me throughout my life, and I have often tried without success to understand why she acted that way. My mother also frequently ranted about how wrong premarital sex was and how disgusted and enraged she would be if she found that either my sister or were engaging in it. I have questioned whether this was a result of her upbringing or her religious beliefs, and whilst it might be true to say that some other women of her generation and background were similarly opposed to premarital sex, my mother's opposition was far more extreme, irrational and rigid. She had no reasoning behind her ingrained thinking, other than it was wrong and she 'hated it' but she couldn't offer any logical explanation for thinking this way.

My sister and I were very used to our mother's rants, outbursts and sometimes violent tantrums as they had always been features of our family life, but they reached new heights when I was about fourteen. I came home from school one day to find my father home from work early, and my mother totally out of control and distraught, loudly weeping and wailing. I could only think that someone had died, but the reason for the drama was shrouded in a secrecy which I was not to be allowed to be privy to. Dramatic rows and scenes were common in our house, and I lived with a low level of anxiety, 'treading on eggshells' for most of my life, trying to mediate between warring family members whilst simultaneously trying to restore calm and prevent my mother from having one of her outbursts, or alternatively finding myself in the thick of the battle. This, however, was of epic proportions and on a different scale to anything I had previously experienced. I sensed that it had something to do with my sister and kept a low profile until bedtime and then spent a sleepless night fearing the worst, until begging my father the next day, to let me know what had happened as the facts couldn't possibly be worse than what I was imagining. Over the next few weeks, I learned that my father had some condoms which he apparently didn't use and was keeping in his wardrobe for someone else. I still think that this is a very peculiar and unbelievable tale, but whatever the real reason for him having these condoms, the crisis had arisen because some of them had gone missing. My parents were concerned about this disappearance and because there were teenage girls in the house, my mother had gone on one of her searches whilst I was in school. Her search unearthed a used condom hidden somewhere in my sister's room. Why my sister hadn't got rid of the thing, I will never know, except that she was a hoarder, but the outcome was that my mother fell apart immediately and walked the streets crying and praying until she found where my father was working. He then immediately left work and took her home. That my mother found him was itself a miracle as my father was working as a meter reader for the electricity board and usually covered the villages surrounding the town at this time, and my mother was convinced that her prayers had been answered. My sister was not a child but was eighteen and was in a stable relationship with the man who she later married but my mother couldn't manage her emotional reaction and there followed a three month 'meltdown' of the grandest scale imaginable. The situation was escalated and catastrophised so that my mother didn't stop crying and couldn't go out, referring to it continually as 'another nail in her coffin'. My father tried to be reasonable in his consoling of her and thought that she might find it less unacceptable if he explained to her that my sister was an adult and that she and her boyfriend were in love, but my mother was totally inconsolable for the whole of this period. She lectured me repeatedly, between weeping and wailing, and threatened me with taking Owain to court for statutory rape if she ever found out that we had been having sex. Another threat that she often directed at me was that if I ever became pregnant, I would be sent away to a Salvation Army unmarried mothers' home and I would be forced to have the baby adopted. This, together with the awareness of the lengths that my mother would go to breach my privacy and catch me out, terrified me for the rest of my time at home, and I dealt with it in the only way that I knew how to: I became very skilled at concealing the truth, from her and my father.

There is another element to this story which I kept secret and felt guilt about for over fifty years. As a child, I used to like rummaging through my parent's wardrobes, trying on old clothes and hats and in one of my rummages, quite a few years before the above incident I found a box of small green and white envelopes with the word Checker written on them in red. Inside one of them I found what I thought were very thin rolled up balloons. I was fascinated with their seeming fragility and texture, and I had great fun first unrolling one and then playing with a couple of them, blowing them up and letting them go. I also discovered that they made good water bombs, so I filled a few of them in the bathroom and played with them over the bath. Anyone who has done this will know that they are surprisingly strong despite their seeming fragility, but they did of course eventually burst, and I threw them away. I didn't tell anyone about this and washed my hands thoroughly to get rid of the disliked smell of rubber and I didn't get found out. Of course, I didn't know what these fragile balloons were at the time that I had played with them, and I'd forgotten about the fun I'd had in the years before the 'incident', so I didn't connect these with my mother's find. I later remembered this and connected it with the missing condoms and have since wondered if I was to blame for my mother's search and the scene which followed. My mother did not allow my sister to wear a white dress on her wedding day because of this and I have carried a burden of guilt ever since. Incidentally, when in his eighties, my father told me that he thought that my mother must have been unable to conceive after I was born as they had never used condoms because he didn't like them. I wish that I had asked him about the box in his wardrobe, but I didn't, and this puzzle will therefore remain forever unsolved. Perhaps he had really been keeping them for someone else, after all.

My mother continued this unreasonable fixation with pre-marital sex throughout her life, choosing to think that I was a virgin when I got married at the age of twenty-four. The night before my wedding, my father teased her about this, saying 'you don't think that she's still a virgin, do you Gwyneth?', to which she replied: 'I don't know and after tomorrow I don't care'. I always thought that this statement summed up the illogicality of her reasoning.

This fixation of hers increased, following my sister's exposé, and together with the need that both my parents had to control me was the main factor in my desperate need to escape and leave home as soon as I possibly could, with the intention of never returning. I realise now that this is not unusual for children of autistic parents. Tony Attwood in the Complete Guide to Asperger's Syndrome, lists leaving home as soon as possible, 'preferably some distance away', as a coping mechanism for children of autistic parents and this was certainly true for me. He also says that children often feel intense hate for the autistic parent but that when that adult child recognises that their parent is autistic, they can begin to understand the parent's personalities, abilities, and motivations better, and can then love and accept the parent, without further hurt. Whilst I don't think that I ever hated my mother I did dislike her intensely for many years, and it is true that recognising that she was autistic was a means to me forgiving and understanding her and subsequently repairing our relationship during the later years of her life.

Despite my intentions of never ever living 'at home' again, I returned to live with my parents when I was unexpectantly and traumatically thrown into the world of single parenthood at the age of twenty-eight. When I was twenty weeks pregnant with my first child, my husband left me for a woman who he had just met and my vulnerability, together with my sister's simple comment of 'come home', joined with my 'hiraeth' and drew me back. My mother's matter of fact, and unemotional reaction to my situation and emotional turmoil provided the support which I needed at that time, and she was my rock throughout the remainder of my pregnancy. I lived with my parents for about eight months and almost succumbed to my father's intense pressure to make a home there for myself and my daughter. Thankfully, I recognised my mother's inability to give me any freedom and my father's desire to house me close to the family home, coupled with his seemingly lack of empathy and need to cast blame on me for the break-down of my marriage, as main indicators of their need to once again 'control' and restrain me. I was able to resist the immense pressure to stay in my uncomfortable, comfort zone and I returned to the safety and freedom of life as a single parent in my own home, which was over three hundred miles away in Kingston-Upon-Hull. My mother however, continued her obsession with sex, and even when I met the man who is now my second husband took every opportunity to shamelessly interrogate my three-year-old daughter in her attempt to find out what we were 'getting up to'.

My father was much more reasonable and rational than my mother, but as I've indicated was not innocent of all responsibility for my unhappiness and desperation to leave home as he too was extremely controlling. His need to control me was however quite different to my mother's as he wanted to control my thinking as well as how I looked and how I reacted. This is still, at the age of sixty-eight painful for me to acknowledge and express as I recognise that I had a passionate love hate relationship with him. Most of the time, I idolised him and his death in 2009 rocked my life with an intensity of grief which I would never have imagined. I still miss him daily and I selfishly regret that he didn't outlive my mother so that I could have enjoyed some time with him, without my mother's intrusion and demands. I have had to acknowledge though that he had a side to him that was hurtful and damaging to my teenage self, and that is both painful and hateful.

I struggled for much of my life with my parents' label of 'rebel' for me, as this is something that I don't identify with, but I recognise that I could not, and still cannot allow anyone to tell me how I should think or respond to others. Any sentence prefixed with the phrase 'what you want to do is', is guaranteed, even now to trigger a negative defensive response in me which I have to consciously work to control, and I suspect that this resistance was a particularly difficult trait for my father to deal with. The result was that we clashed regularly on topics ranging from something as mundane as the temperature outside, to more significant ones such as what someone said, decision making, or our differing interpretations and responses to the Sunday sermon. In our family any disagreements resulted in the vociferous and ruthless hurling of personalised verbal abuse at each other, and extremely hurtful things were said on both sides, making Sundays anything but a day of peace and rest. There were few people in my father's life whom he respected, and I think that this may have been a problem which was rooted deeply in something from his past, but I did manage to earn his respect later in my life, after gaining two degrees and successfully publishing two books, and these heated arguments were eventually replaced with controlled, and sometimes deep discussions, particularly about politics and faith in which we mostly shared similar views. His attacks on my teenage looks, however, were much more damaging to me and my self-image and were significantly more difficult for me to deal with, having a lasting effect on my perception of myself and who I am. These attacks took the form of constant criticism.

The most predominant target for my father's criticism was my hair. In a recent reunion with friends from my youth, two of them commented on how as a teenager I had 'beautiful thick, long, blonde hair'. I cannot express the degree of shock and disbelief that I experienced on hearing this, as whilst I agreed that my hair was long, I genuinely believed that it was 'thin, mousy and greasy'. This comment challenged me to question my views and I found a couple of photographs from this period, which very surprisingly to me supported my friends' comments. It seems that my father's opinion was so instilled and ingrained in me that I still believed him, even into my sixties.

When 'flower power' hit Llanelli in the 1960s, the fashion was for young women to grow their hair to one length, with a centre, or slightly off centre, side parting. I had no idea of how to style myself at this time, but this generic, easy to manage hair style appealed to me as it meant that I no longer had to endure visits to the hairdresser and live with the predictably bad haircut, but it also enabled me to exert some control over my appearance and identity. Growing a short, layered hair style with a fringe, to a one length style is time consuming and challenging, at best. The internet is now full of advice on nutrition, vitamin supplements, techniques and haircare to attempt to ease and hasten the process but such advice was not available to my 1960s teenage self. Time, patience and endurance were required to live through the difficult and awkward interim 'no style' period and given that hair grows approximately only a half an inch a month, a great deal of these qualities was required. It took me about eighteen months to two years to grow my hair to the length I desired and during this period I was subjected to unrelenting criticism from my father. He bombarded me daily with negative comments about my hair: it 'was awful'; it 'made me look dirty', and he was 'ashamed of me every time he looked at me'. He constantly told me that 'a woman's hair is her crowning glory' and that mine did not come up to this standard. Sundays were the worst as I had to put my hair up, in what I confess was quite a severe, virtually Victorian style to comply with the

Salvation Army uniform regulations, and my seat in the Songsters put me directly in his line of vision throughout the meeting. I had to endure his criticism during every Sunday dinner for at least a year until I bought a wig to wear under my bonnet which solved the problem: for Sundays' at least. I don't quite know how I stood up to the relentless attacks, but I refused to have my hair cut and fought a long and hard battle which involved many tears and arguments in order to retain my long, straight locks. I was rigidly stubborn in my determination to grow my hair and this aspect of my character won the battle, but my confidence and self-esteem was severely wounded in the process. My self-image was at rock bottom, and I have struggled for the whole of my life to improve this. I still wonder how my father, who I know loved me, could have been so vicious and cruel in his attack.

My hair wasn't the only target for criticism: there was also my relationship with Owain and the clothes which he and I wore. The first problem that my father had with Owain started because he didn't take me home to meet his parents, and my father was unable to control my thinking on this issue. Whilst I wanted to meet Owain's parents, I fully understood his reasoning for this. Owain was what was commonly referred to as 'an afterthought'. He was born when his mother was in her early forties and had a much older brother and sister. He had seen both of his siblings marry and have children and whilst his parents weren't interfering, he was well aware, with an emotional maturity far greater than mine, that relationships do not take place in isolation and that they have emotional ramifications for other family members. Both his parents loved their son-in-law and daughter-in-law, and Owain was acutely aware in the early days, of how upset they would be if they also grew to love me, and our relationship didn't last. He talked about relationships being like pebbles being thrown into a pond, with ripples extending far beyond them, and involving others, and he didn't want to take me home, at that time, precisely because of this. Somewhat ironically, he did take me home after about three years, and I loved his parents and his mother certainly loved me, but our relationship didn't last for ever. I regret, and I'm not proud of how I ended it and I think his mother was very hurt and upset by it. Owain's reasoning, however, just didn't fit with my father's comprehension of how relationships worked and how I should be treated, and he handled it very badly. Instead of talking to Owain about it, he nagged me constantly and he couldn't understand how I was accepting of it or how his comments were hurting me. His main voiced concern was that he thought that Owain was ashamed of me hence his unwillingness to take me to meet his parents. No amount of my arguing and tearful pleading with him to recognise that this wasn't the case had any impact on his ability to empathise with either Owain's feelings or mine and this was just another weapon which he used relentlessly to attack me, and of course, my self-esteem. I still don't know why he didn't communicate his worries to Owain instead of me, except that he wasn't good at communicating emotions, but his constant nagging and suggestions that Owain was ashamed of me made me feel worthless and did nothing to improve my already fragile self-esteem.

Owain was an artist and an excellent photographer who took a sketch pad and a camera everywhere with him and he liked to use me as his model, or muse. He photographed me in all sorts of places and in all states of dress: swinging from branches of big trees in the local park or throwing water in the air in one of our local rivers or just sitting in leafy settings with interesting lighting or against interesting backgrounds. One of my mother's lifelong passions was taking 'snaps' and she thought that she was an excellent photographer because her photographs were always centred and in focus. Her method of photography however couldn't have been more different to Owain's: she would line people up against the nearest wall as if they were in front of a firing squad, and then take the required picture. This in itself wasn't a problem, but her and my father's fixed and rigid attitude towards photography was. Neither of them had the ability to see any artistic merit and they (particularly my father) mocked and made fun of those photographs of Owain's which they were allowed to see, taunting me about them and expecting me to agree with their views. My father in particular was very persistent and vociferous in his mocking and negative comments, trying to coerce me into thinking the same way about the photos as he did. Of course, I didn't, and once again he didn't discuss any of this with Owain who would have been able to enlighten him from a technical and artistic perspective. I realise now that my father had no interest in that type of discussion as the main purpose of his tirades was to try to persuade me to his way of thinking. It did of course have the opposite effect!

Owain's homelife was very different to mine. His parents were much older and were relaxed and happy with him and each other. Very differently to my parents, they allowed him to be himself. Owain's mother was a talented craftswoman and seamstress. She knitted, crocheted and sewed for all of the family and also for members of her local community. She made all of Owain's clothes, according to his designs and specifications. Owain was creative, he knew who he was and wasn't worried about being it, and this was seen in his adventurous choice of clothes which reflected an up to the minute fashion which had not yet reached Llanelli. I, on the other hand was the opposite of this and needed to 'find myself'. He encouraged me to be more daring in my dress sense, and his birthday and Christmas gifts reflected his artistic and sometimes eccentric style, often causing me huge anxiety when anticipating my parents' reaction to them. He bought horse brasses and leather thongs and made me a pendant necklace with them which I treasured and always wore; he also bought me a wonderful black hooded Indian caftan covered with vibrant colourful embroidery, which I also loved and in 1971, when he went to London for his interview at University, he visited Carnaby Street and bought me the most fashionable tiny, blue, velvet hot pants, which incidentally I still treasure, although they haven't fitted me for many years. He himself wore a red satin shirt with a big collar and sleeves which his mother made, but also wore a large ex-military camouflage jacket on a daily basis. He turned heads wherever we went, in what I thought was a backward thinking Welsh town and I loved and embraced his difference but had to learn how to not be embarrassed by people's reactions to him. My parents however made no attempt to embrace or accommodate anything and my sometimes unrelenting, verbatim memory means that my father's negative comments about me and Owain are forever imprinted in my mind.

In all fairness, I didn't have many clothes (we didn't then), and I didn't dress unconventionally most of the time. As already mentioned, I wore school uniform for five days of the week and then Salvation Army uniform on a Sunday. My preferred image was loons (a style of trousers) or jeans and a tee shirt, with a very long cardigan which Owain's mother had knitted for me, although I did wear my horse brasses necklace and very occasionally a leather thong as a head band. I still however earned the reputation of being a rebel, a label which I eventually learnt to embrace and be proud of as my parents continued to attribute it to me throughout the whole of their lives. When I got a tattoo at the age of forty, I realised that secretly my father enjoyed this aspect of my character as he was very amused by my tattoo and unlike my mother, admired it. This may of course be because it was of a daffodil and in choosing this, I was also embracing my Welshness, after living in England for more than twenty years. I will never really know, because in many respects my father was a closed book. I have often wondered if he too was autistic as there were certain aspects of his character which fitted the diagnostic criteria. He was an excellent communicator in formal situations but in others seemed to shy away from challenges and he definitely struggled to empathise in what is the predominately neuro-typical male way. He also had the gift of oversharing: when he was well in his eighties, as well as telling me that he hadn't used condoms, he also told me that he was convinced that he didn't experience prostrate trouble because he had always indulged in regular sex – too much information for his daughter to hear! He also had many executive functioning difficulties which is why he didn't achieve academically but had persevered to overcome or develop strategies for these. He was forced to write with his right hand, being naturally left-handed and I have toyed at times with the idea of possible Dyspraxia, ADHD, Dyslexia, or atypical autism diagnoses, but I cannot identify any specific label which I would be comfortable to attach to him. His life experiences affected him greatly and fighting on the front line during the war had a huge impact, as did living with my mother's demands. He also became a Christian in 1958 after studying as a Marxist atheist to prove that there was no God, and this changed him significantly. All of these things make it difficult to know what the 'real man' behind the mask was, so 'different' is perhaps the label that best suits him although in my teenage years I thought that all fathers were like him.

There was another side to our relationship which I loved: I have said that my father was born at least one generation too soon and I've indicated that at a different time he would have found his vocation through a career in law. My mother prevented this as he was given the opportunity to study in Cardiff after the war, but she could not countenance either moving or being without him during the week. He was a self-educated man, and his knowledge was limited to areas of his special interests but after becoming a Christian, he focused his intellect on the Bible and social justice. He became a Biblical scholar par excellence and bored me with his endless Biblical exegeses, and he also studied employment law so that he could represent colleagues who had been unfairly treated by their employer. In the early years, after his Christian conversion, he was asked to lead a Youth Group in the Salvation Army, which he loved and later, when I was a teenager, he was asked to take on the leadership of a youth group which combined Biblical Study with youth activities. He related well to the youth, and everyone loved him. Just recently, the same friends who complimented me on my hair, told me how wonderful they thought my father was and were in disbelief when I told them how I suffered from his criticism, but the truth is that he was complex: he was both critical and fun to be with; he was both loving and unkind. He encouraged us to do exciting things like all night sponsored walks and have real barbeques in local woods. He even, to my huge embarrassment, joined in with the lads who urinated on the fire at the end of the evening to ensure that it was completely extinguished. He also welcomed people to our home, persuading my mother to decorate the front room when I was about fourteen, so that I was able to bring friends home. He also embarrassed me hugely at these times, as most fathers do, with his unrelenting unfunny and repetitive sense of humour.

Like me, my father was a Christian Socialist. I have learnt and accepted that he had many demons and that he could never have been the perfect father that I wanted. The Christian faith is after all not for perfect people and we are all damaged by the physical and emotional hurts of the challenge that is life. My father sought to combine the lifestyle teachings of Jesus with his political beliefs, both of which challenge injustice, advocate equality and seek to save the lost and the broken. He tried to do this with love and humility, but he sometimes failed, because he was human. He continued to learn, throughout his life and I have forgiven him for the hurts that he caused me as

I know that he did his best with the emotional tools that he had at the time. He taught me many things, but most of all I am grateful to him for teaching me about justice, equality and inclusion and that 'there but for the grace of God go I'.

Despite his faults, he was a loving and caring father.

To my Father
If you were here now
I would tell you how much I love you
And how much I miss you
I would tell you how your criticisms hurt
and how I have forgiven you.

If you were here now
I would thank you for what you taught me
I would watch the Rugby with you
We would talk politics late into the night
And we would sing together

If you were here now
We would laugh together
I would ask you more about your childhood
We would go for a drive together
And you would teach me all that you learnt.
If only you were here now.

CHAPTER 7

The long road to recognition

It took me fifty years to recognise that my mother was autistic: I spent the first twenty of these learning the basics of autism; the following thirty years provided a continuous refining of that knowledge and understanding through sharing, listening, and questioning my acquired knowledge with autistic people.

In Chapter 1 I described the development of my professional interest and career in autism which started when I was in my early twenties, and which has continued to be my passion and career path throughout my life. I have described how I have always been attracted to unusual and 'different' people. From a young child I was known as a 'defender of the underdog' and this not only influenced my professional, but also my personal life. In the summer of 1972, I met someone who was more different to anyone who I had previously encountered, and I didn't like him one little bit. This was a university friend of my boyfriend Owain who, visited us with a friend of his, unexpectedly in our hometown during the summer holidays of 1972. Both were arrogant and disrespectful, with a level of egocentrism, accompanied by insensitivity and self-absorption which I hadn't previously encountered. They took great delight in mocking Welsh culture and traditions, and they were rude and ungrateful to Owain's mother (who had been very welcoming to them), mocking her hospitality and making fun of the tinned stuffed pork roll which she had used in the sandwiches which she prepared for their return journey to Yorkshire. They had what I thought was a peculiar habit of adopting odd physical walks and postures and shrieking very loudly in public places, which they found hilarious; a sentiment which wasn't shared or understood by anyone else, least of all me. I found them and their behaviour both embarrassing and intolerable and I disliked them immensely. I met Owain's friend again in the autumn of 1972, after I had moved to Chislehurst and was visiting Owain in Woolwich, and over time, my immense dislike for him changed to interest and intrigue.

Eddy (as he was called) had a wealthy, well-educated and privileged background which I would describe as vaguely bohemian and intellectual, and which was diametrically opposed to mine. He was the second of five children in a family which had experienced a personal loss and grief which impacted hugely on all family members and altered the direction of their lives. He openly and factually stated that he was emotionally damaged, calling himself 'an emotional cripple' and 'insecure'. At the age of twenty, he had experienced a number of romantic relationships, none of which he had found fulfilling. I have often, over the years, wondered if I was drawn to him because he was autistic, but I don't think that he would meet the diagnostic criteria, and in view of this, and given that he had excellent neurotypical communication skills, I have concluded that he was an emotionally damaged person who lacked emotional and compassionate empathy, as well as a moral compass. I knew him for about four years during which time I was working in the childcare sector. I had moved from the East End Reception and Assessment Centre to work in an ILEA residential school for 'Maladjusted Boys', a term which is thankfully no longer used but in retrospect was clearly a pre-autism spectrum term for neurodiversity, including autism and ADHD. This was extremely emotionally challenging and draining; my long-term relationship was in difficulties as we had developed diverging interests and were growing apart and I found myself fascinated and seduced by this man's intellect, creativity and difference, as well as his reckless and care-free attitude to life. I was socially, emotionally and intellectually naive and vulnerable, and what little resistance I had was futile as I was overwhelmed by intrigue, passion, and a desire to help him. We married in 1977, after an intense and tumultuous courtship, some aspects of which I'm not proud of, and I followed him to Kingston-Upon-Hull, where I supported him emotionally and financially to study Architecture and I, after a short period of unemployment became a Social Worker. Once again, I found that I was working with teenagers, predominantly girls, many of whom were school refusers who had been groomed by older men, and some of whom I would in retrospect suggest might have received a diagnosis of Asperger Syndrome, if it had been known about at that time.

I have mentioned briefly that I became a single parent in 1981. This intense, volatile marriage was doomed to failure and Eddy left me after three years for another woman, whom he had recently met. I was twenty weeks pregnant with my first child, at the time and I was devastated but I wasn't really surprised, as I was always aware that he and I didn't share the same moral code. With forty years of hindsight, I think that I had thought that I might have been able to assist his emotional development, particularly in the area of emotional and compassionate empathy, but our seven-year relationship had no impact on this. The breakdown of my marriage in these heart-breaking circumstances triggered a ten-year career break during which time I raised my daughter; was diagnosed with ulcerative colitis; married the man who is now my husband of thirty-six years; moved to Sheffield; gave birth to my second daughter; reconsidered my options, and finally, returned to study. My older daughter was discovered to be Dyslexic and that, together with my love of people watching led me to think that I should study Psychology. I was awarded a place at the University of Sheffield, but during the UCAS application process discovered that the then relatively recent academic discipline of Communication Studies suited me much better, so in 1989, to everyone's shock and some people's horror, I enrolled on the BA Hons course in Communication Studies at what was then Sheffield City Polytechnic. Many people, including my parents, questioned how I could turn down a place at a red brick university for one in a polytechnic, but having never been status conscious, this wasn't a consideration for me. I am forever thankful that I made this decision as without doubt, this course changed the direction of my life forever.

The Communication Studies degree provided the first opportunity for me to study Autism, Dyslexia and Deafness, at an academic level, under the broader module name of 'Communication Disorders' and this ignited an enduring lifelong passion in me for communication and more specifically autism, and once again, the rest is history!

I have always found studying difficult as I have some executive functioning difficulties particularly in the areas of working memory and organisation and my grammar school education neglected to teach me study skills, assuming I would either already have these or pick them up along the way. Whilst I learnt to read easily at the age of three and a half and am an excellent mechanical reader, I find reading for understanding to be excruciatingly difficult so academic reading is exhausting for me. I discovered however, that I had an intuitive knowledge and understanding of autism so that I didn't have to work hard at it: I just seemed to absorb knowledge. I learnt without knowing how, and I devoured everything that I could find to read. I was so enthusiastic to learn more that I was one of the first people to enrol on Sheffield Hallam University's new Master's degree in Autism, which I studied for and completed whilst I was working full time. I was always (and still am) drawn to autobiographical accounts of autism, with Donna Williams (aka Polly Samuel) becoming my all-time autism 'guru', and I firmly and passionately believe that whilst academic knowledge has its place, autistic people are the experts in this field, teaching us more on the subject than a library of academic books can. Our role in the intellectual exchange is to be willing to find a way to listen and hear from them. From my undergraduate degree onwards, I was hooked and all my career choices since then were guided by increasing the development of my autism knowledge and skills, with the continued desire and intention of working in the field of autism.

In 2006, I wrote The Autism Spectrum and Further Education – a guide to good practice which in many ways was the accumulation of my life's knowledge and expertise **at that point in time**. Page 43 of this book, records how people had often criticised me for being ideological and idealistic and records how I countered this negative criticism by stating that it was directed at what I consider to be positive attributes; choosing to view the search for high ideals and having high aims for professional practice as essential factors in enabling us to find the 'perfect model' to imitate. My knowledge and understanding of autism have thankfully moved on since then, but I stand by that principle. This has been challenging over the intervening years and has required many soul-searching moments in my life, the biggest of which involved moving from the financial security of a well-paid job to the uncertainty of breaking out and setting up on my own: all because I was ideological and idealistic! I am so thankful that I am, because without ideas, beliefs and striving for perfection (whilst recognising that it may be unattainable), I would not have taken the huge leap of faith at the end of 2003 to set up Spectrum First Ltd. Without striving for perfection, I doubt if I would have continued learning, and working independently, with autistic people, which enabled me to follow my fundamental core beliefs: that essentially, we learn most about autism from autistic people and that good practice requires us to not only include the autistic voice and follow a person centred and autism specific approach, but to put these at the centre of all of our practice. Working independently also freed me from the constraints, restrictions and bureaucracy which inevitably accompanies working for an organisation, and which limited my creativity. It was not my intention at the time to become an employer and I didn't imagine that I would set up a company which would eventually employ twenty-eight staff, who would support many hundreds of university students, using the ideals and approach that I advocated. I also didn't realise that this leap of faith would be the means of restoration and reconciliation of my relationship with my mother through providing the pathway for me to eventually recognise that she was, indeed, autistic.

At this point, I had completed many non-clinical autism assessments for people who wanted some confirmation and reassurance before seeking and paying for a formal autism diagnosis and I prided myself in having an unbroken record of accuracy in this area. I was also free to pick and choose my work, and my belief that there was insufficient support for adult autistic people, which led to the setting up of Spectrum First Ltd, was confirmed so that I had no shortage of work.

In 2004 I was persuaded via The National Autistic Society, to provide independent autism specialist advocacy for a man who coincidentally lived just two streets away from my parents in my hometown of Llanelli. What I didn't realise when I agreed to this was that the experience was to be my 'road to Damascus' in terms of removing my blindness and enabling me to recognise that my mother was indeed autistic.

My view of independent advocacy is that it is the most challenging area of support to provide. My experience is that autistic adults who seek me out to advocate for them are desperate. They have lived their lives in a society which favours and prioritises the predominant neurotype at the expense of all others, and they have suffered from prejudice and discrimination throughout their lives. In addition, many have arrived at a diagnosis later in life after being mislabelled, targeted, bullied and misunderstood, not only by their peers and neighbours, but also by those organisations and institutions which society has put in place to protect and support them. They have often been failed by education, childcare and mental health services as well as Social Services and the criminal justice system. As a result, they find themselves living on the edge of society's acceptable boundaries, often in poverty and isolation, having suffered major breakdowns in health as well as family and working relationships. They have typically been vociferous in their attempts to speak for themselves, but they have not been listened to, or their views and behaviours have been inaccurately interpreted, and they have been given the labels of 'habitual complainant' or been banned from accessing services as they have been mislabelled as being 'unreasonable', 'demanding' and 'aggressive' in their search for answers and support. In many cases, autistic people have been inappropriately diagnosed as having a personality disorder or another psychiatric illness or additional personality disorders, and their persistence in challenging these inaccurate labels has been used against them as evidence and justification for that labelling. All of these had been this man's experience when he sought advocacy support in his fifties.

Autism advocacy is draining and exhausting: it requires time, patience and understanding to revisit painful and traumatic experiences, as well as an in-depth practical knowledge of autism accompanied by the skills to listen, interpret and counsel people: all of this is needed whilst also providing a non-judgemental and unbiased representation of the autistic person and their views. It involves many hours of compassionate and empathetic, active listening, explaining, questioning, and often trawling through reams of paperwork in order to tease out information in the hope of arriving at an accurate understanding of the person's thoughts, feelings and opinions so that they can be communicated objectively to others. In this instance, the length and complexity of the situation plus the continued onslaught of pressure from society's institutions and organisations, including the courts, required a number of years of my involvement. Over this time, I found that I was not only teasing out the differences, misunderstandings and conflicts between autistic and neurotypical understanding, but this bi-lingual, Welsh and English-speaking man was also teaching me more about Welsh identity and culture and was enabling me to tease out the differences between what it was to be Welsh and what it was to be autistic. During this process, I began to see numerous similarities in his and my mother's communication and behaviour, and slowly, the recognition that other Welsh people were challenging this man's autistic identity enabled me to recognise that what were viewed by others as 'challenging behaviours' had nothing to do with him and my mother being Welsh, and working class, but had everything to do with them being autistic in a neuro-typical world.

The saying "pride goes before a fall" was a reality for me and I was both astonished and ashamed that I had not previously recognised that my mother was so obviously autistic, but more than that, I was ashamed that I had chosen and preferred to use the negative labels for her, the same labels which I so readily as a professional challenged in others. The fact that I had wrongly labelled my mother as a 'difficult Welsh woman' who we had to 'tread on eggshells' around, when in fact she was an autistic Welsh woman was a shocking revelation to me and I did not accept it without a certain level of guilt and feelings of shame and hypocrisy. I should have recognised it sooner, and I will always regret this, but this Damascene moment was the means to understanding and reconciliation in what had up until then been a very uncomfortable relationship. I did find some comfort in the knowledge that this was also the experience of Professor Tony Attwood who is a much more highly regarded autism specialist than I am.

Despite the recognition and revelation, I still had to 'tread on eggshells' and I continue to question why the realisation took me so long.

Why did it take me so long?

Why did it take me so long
To see what was so close to me?
Why didn't I see it before
When it was so clear and so obvious?
Was I blind
Or was I like those who will not see?
Was it the defeat of resistance or the acquisition
of knowledge
Which led me there?

CHAPTER 8

Revelation and realisation

I have always been good at recognising autistic people: it's just something that I'm able to do as it seems I am drawn to them or perhaps have some sort of intuitive radar, a type of gift which is effortless. This combined with my professional experienced and academic learning made 'assessing' my mother's autism relatively easy. I chose to follow a formal route for my assessment (if I could call it that, as I make no claims to being a diagnostician), sticking closely to the diagnostic criteria, as I was keen to distance myself from my subjective opinions. As a result, it proved to be quite detailed, and it forms the longest chapter in this book. I worried about this when writing it and I have looked for ways to break it up but on completion I decided that there was no alternative, and that I should make no apologies for it. This chapter is the beating heart of the book as it describes my mother's autism and how my recognition of it led to an understanding which was a means of saving our relationship and reconciling what might otherwise have been lost forever. I am who I am, and I do what I do, partly because of my mother's Autism but that is the subject for later discussion.

Childhood History

Firstly, despite my mother being seventy-six years of age when I began my unofficial assessment of her in 2014, I had relatively easy access to her childhood history some of which I had been aware of throughout my life. I did however also have to rely on her recollections as well as anecdotal evidence which had previously been shared by those who knew her. I also ran through a standard Childhood Questionnaire which is often used as a precursor for autism diagnosis in girls. Even the limited evidence which this generated began to indicate autism, so my sister and I then completed the Autism Quotient (AQ) Test together, basing our answers on our knowledge of our mother. This achieved the score of 45 which would have been more than sufficient to indicate the need for a formal diagnostic assessment if desired.

Pre diagnostic questionnaires typically ask for details of difficulties during birth: I have already mentioned that my mother was born, weighing just shy of fourteen pounds, after a prolonged and difficult three-day labour. I think it would be accurate to judge this as a traumatic birth for both mother and child. I was unable to find any information of her early years, but an objective investigation of her childhood would suggest that it wasn't typical for the time. She was described as an extremely sensitive child who was sheltered and protected throughout her childhood and teenage years by a formidable mother who defended her and fought her corner on all counts. Knowing my grandmother's courageous and down to earth attitude to life and remembering how she related to me and my sister, this suggests that she knew that her daughter needed protecting. There is evidence that she had communication difficulties: she was described as shy, withdrawn and a 'wall flower'; she had a limited vocabulary; she rigidly refused to speak Welsh despite it being the language of the home and her recollection was that she would hide from people and run home if anyone outside of the home tried to speak to her. She didn't understand humour or teasing, suggesting that she took language literally and she was described as a loner who was 'afraid of her shadow'. There is also a suggestion of inflexible behaviour in that she disliked changes to her routine.

My mother clearly had sensory differences as a child, and these were mostly evidenced in her dislike of certain smells, noises and her fussy or 'faddy' eating which has already been described in some detail in Chapter 2. She also disliked being touched or getting dirty and she preferred solitary play. I would also attribute her dislike of hearing her own voice when reading aloud to being possibly related to a sensory difference. It's not unusual to dislike the sound of one's recorded voice, but I think that the degree of my mother's dislike of hearing herself speak may have been extreme, suggesting that it was more than typical. She also told of excruciating pain when for some reason a Scottish bagpiper would visit her street. She recalled that the intensity of pain was such that she would run to the room furthest away from the sound and bury her head in as may pillows as she could find.

Recollections of school were that she was a loner who didn't take part in activities and who was prone to emotional outbursts and melt downs. She hid from attention and demands, running home if any were made of her. My understanding is that she didn't play in the same way as other children did and used toys and dolls more as ornaments than playthings; something which she also expected of her children. She could read well but never read books, preferring to read maps. She loved numbers and excelled at mental arithmetic but was unable to demonstrate this in verbal classroom tests.

These recollections and anecdotal evidence were useful in identifying a number of potentially 'autistic traits', but my unofficial assessment of her as autistic, relied, of necessity on my lifetime's observations, with some confirmation from my sister, together with retrospective interpretations gained from my professional knowledge and experience.

My Lifelong Recollections and Observations

I was aware from a young age that my sister and I shared the role of protecting, supporting and looking after our mother when our father was absent, but I wasn't aware that this was different to any other child's experience. Looking after my mother centred on reducing her anxiety, keeping her calm, and preventing her from embarrassing us by bursting into tears or running away. We learned to do this by primarily anticipating situations which were potentially stressful for her and using diversion tactics to avoid them. When we were unable to avoid situations, we would either put ourselves forward in her place or would interpret others' meanings and intensions for her, often speaking for her in any unwanted social interactions. Travelling on buses was difficult for my mother and my retrospective analysis and discussion with her suggests that it was one of the main reasons for her insistence on moving back to be closer to the town centre, as she was always worried about the practicalities of flagging the bus down and not getting off at the right stop. In retrospect, I also realised that her shopping habits ensured minimal anxiety from unplanned conversations with people: the corner shop was a precursor of internet shopping where she would take her written weekly list and receive the delivery at a certain time on the Friday evening; unavoidable trips to the town centre for clothes, shoes or other provisions were always accompanied by either me or my sister, when we would speak to the shop assistants on her behalf; she rigidly stuck to visiting only certain shops where she and her mother were well known and refused to shop in the excellent market where there was banter and conversation with stall holders, some of whom might only speak Welsh. In retrospect, I realised that these were the coping strategies which enabled her to maintain her pride and dignity in what were incredibly stressful situations for her. I remember that throughout her life she was unable to return any wrongly bought item, despite having help to prepare and practice scripts for the return process. This was of course because of the uncertainty of the situation and the fear of not knowing how she would respond to an unexpected comment or a possible refusal. Incidentally, this is also something that I find difficult, but my sister and I took on this responsibility for her and I learned how to perform it by taking on a character, in the same way as I would do when acting in a play. I also remember how, when walking arm in arm with my mother my role was to scan the street, spotting people in advance to warn her in time to either prepare to acknowledge them, or to employ strategies such as crossing over the road and keeping her head down to prevent eye contact with them, or similarly, to avoid strangers who she might find intimidating. She also had a particular anxiety of anyone who might have been drinking alcohol. In retrospect I realised that this was because the potential for them to be chatty and unpredictable was high, so I was also required to spot people coming out of pubs, or whose appearance indicated that they were 'under the influence', enabling us to avoid them by crossing the road. I realise now that this scouting role wasn't every child's experience, but it was perfectly normal for me at the time. Of course, once I revisited these experiences as an autism practitioner as opposed to a daughter, I was able to see how successful my mother had been in engaging me and my sister in devising coping strategies which not only helped her but also masked her differences from others.

Working at the Co-op provided another opportunity for my mother to avoid the stresses of a typical weekly supermarket shop as she was able to complete her shopping during a quiet time at work, supported by her exceptional mapping skills of the product placements in the store. On the surface, working in a supermarket, albeit a small one would appear to present challenges for someone with my mother's sensory and communication needs, but she had an extremely understanding manager, who allowed her to work only on the checkout. She loved numbers and counting money and took pride in working at high speed. This ensured that she minimised the opportunities for small talk and banter with customers who were required to focus on matching their packing speed to her checking out speed. She also learnt that checkout conversations followed a similar pattern for all customers, and she was able to learn and repeat the scripts for these. Deviation from the script caused panic and she was always frightened of any customer being challenged for shoplifting as she would not know how to deal with the uncertainty which would accompany it.

My mother had been brought up from birth to worship at the Salvation Army, and this was a rigidly fixed and sometimes irrational routine throughout her life. She professed to have a Christian faith, although found this difficult to articulate and I think this was perhaps superficial for much of her early adult years, although I do believe that there was a deepening of her faith in her later years. As a younger adult, the military styled structure and orderliness of the Salvation Army suited her: as a uniformed member, she didn't have to choose what to wear; she was shy of singing but on her own admission, mimed in the Songsters (choir), which meant that she had an allocated seat in the soprano section for all of the meetings, which followed a regular structure with rules or direct guidance for when to stand, sing and clap, so she was able to maintain the appearance of participation, (although she always chose not to clap). The Salvation Army encourages individuals within the congregation to participate during the meetings, either by praying aloud or reading a verse of a song, and it is not unusual to be asked at random to perform one of these activities. New Corps Officers (ministers) presented particular challenges and anxieties for my mother, as they would not be aware of her difficulties, but they very quickly learnt that she would burst into tears and run out of the hall, if asked to perform either of these tasks, leaving either me or my sister to follow her whilst the other would jump out of their seat to perform the task on her behalf. This strategy which my father, who at this time was not a member of the Salvation Army devised and instructed us in the execution of, worked well, and usually resulted in her not being asked by the same officer twice. Once again, my retrospective analysis enabled me to recognise that this was a form of what Donna Williams calls 'exposure anxiety', which had triggered the flight or fight response, and which could of course be indicative of autism.

Whilst my mother was a competent reader, I never knew her to read a book, but she frequently read knitting patterns; maps, and telephone directories, which she took great pleasure in, priding herself in her knowledge of how many people with certain names lived in our town, as well as her exceptional knitting and map reading skills.

My mother's need for sameness and routine became more obvious as she got older as circumstances required changes to these. Retiring from the Songsters was accompanied by the loss of a specific seat for meetings in the Salvation Army and that, together with no longer wearing the uniform presented new challenges which she addressed by choosing to wear the same clothes (her own uniform) to the weekly meetings and insisting on arriving an hour early to ensure that she could sit in what she had claimed as 'her seat'. Punctuality was essential and if my father wasn't ready at her pre-determined time, then her anxiety would be such that verbal rows would quickly erupt. One on occasion, someone else unknowingly sat in 'her seat' prior to her arrival, so she returned home and from then on, brought forward her arrival time to two hours before the start of the meeting, a feat only made possible by my father having the key and responsibility, for opening the hall. Despite being part of the Salvation Army for her entire life, she was known to everyone but had no real friends. Attempts by others at friendships were often rejected, or if accepted weren't sustained, and no one visited her at home as they were not welcomed. Later in her life, after I had left home, my father was allowed visitors, firstly in the formal rule governed capacity of a home Bible study group, and much later individuals occasionally sought his company for his knowledge and wisdom. My mother's lack of hospitality was difficult for my father as he was very sociable and loved company, but my mother continued to be resentful of these visits and the impact of them on my father's time.

I was by no means the perfect child or carer as I was often irritated and frustrated by my mother's seeming fragility, especially as her outward persona differed from mine, but mostly because it was also very different to that which I encountered at home. At home, my mother 'ruled the roost' with 'an iron hand', and I found her controlling nature difficult to deal with. Being more like my father, I was a bit of a naughty, dare devil child and at times I tested her patience to its limits and experienced her wrath and punishments accordingly. Whilst I learned to read her moods, I also provoked her at times, causing her frustration and meltdowns. I avoided her physical responses to her lack of control by either outwitting and outrunning her, or by concealing the truth from her. She often despaired of me and resorted to waiting until my father got home, to enlist his help in disciplining me. On these occasions I was bewildered by her relating my offending behaviour to my father in a way which didn't match my recollection of what was said or done and for many years I saw this as intentional manipulation of the truth for her own interests and benefit. As a teenager, I labelled her as attention seeking, and a liar and this contributed significantly to my dislike of her which lasted into my adulthood. It was only when I distanced myself and viewed this objectively from an autism perspective that I was able to recognise that there was no intention behind her misconstruction of the facts, but her perception of her external reality was different to mine. In recognising this, I also began to realise that this must also be true of her internal experiences and reality.

In terms of perception, my mother's differed to most other people's in almost every aspect. She perceived touch differently and all her physical contact was very heavy handed and rough but conversely and confusingly, she also loved very gentle stroking which I would describe as light tickling. I always seemed to have cuts on my knees as a child, and I always thought that there was no compassion shown when she scrubbed my legs every morning as part of the morning ablution routine. I tanned easily in the sun, unlike other members of the family, so in the summer months my mother would insist that my neck was dirty, and would scrub it, showing no mercy. Similarly, my hair was combed and tied in a bow with a desire for perfection which gave no consideration or awareness of my pain and discomfort. Temperature was a constant bone of contention in a coalfired, non-centrally heated house and arguments over temperature control were rife in winter months as my mother was always cold. In the summer, blinds had to be drawn in the south facing living room as the sun was always too bright for her comfort. My father called her 'Hawkeye' as her visual perception was so acute that she could spot a discrepancy in pattern or colour which was invisible to others but which she found intolerable, requiring it to be corrected at all costs. She couldn't tolerate the smell of some perfumes, or lilies, which would trigger headaches, and more conventionally unpleasant ones would make her gag or vomit. She also hated high pitched or repetitive sounds which would trigger melt downs and refused to go to the dentist because of the noise of the drill. She didn't have a filling, preferring at the age of forty to have all of her teeth removed under general anaesthetic in order to minimise the need for further visits, and she insisted that my father always accompanied me and my sister to our appointments as she couldn't tolerate hearing the drill from the waiting room.

My mother also experienced pain differently: she was proud to tell me that she made no sound during childbirth, and I always suspected that she had a different pain threshold to most people. This was confirmed when she fell downstairs, around the time that I was conducting my 'unofficial assessment' of her. One of my chores before I left home in 1972 was to 'set' my mother's hair in a specific style every Saturday evening as she was unable to tolerate visiting a hairdresser. I would also cut and perm it for her every few months or so, as this was something that I seemed to have some skill at. When I left home, she was most insistent on maintaining this routine, so she was forced to find a suitable hairdresser, whom she then visited on a weekly basis, and these visits became one of her rigid routines which could not be altered at any cost. The day that she fell downstairs was, coincidently, the day when she had an appointment with her hairdresser for a perm. Her fall was dramatic, and she was badly injured: she knocked her forehead on the telephone table so severely, that the swelling and bruising extended down the left side of her face and lasted for weeks; she also had multiple fractures in both of her wrists which remained permanently misshapen for the rest of her life.

My father very sensibly wanted to take her to hospital immediately, but she was fixated on keeping her hairdresser appointment and would not be persuaded otherwise. The hairdresser fortunately recognised the severity of her injuries and took control, advising her that the trauma of the fall would prevent the perm from working. She also advised that she visit the Accident and Emergency Department at the local hospital immediately, where it was found that she had been concussed and had fractured both wrists. That autistic people can experience pain differently is well documented, so this seemed to add evidence to my growing understanding of my mother as being autistic.

As an older child and teenager who was an animal lover, I found my mother's hatred of anything furry intolerably frustrating as we had a cat whom I loved, but I had no choice other than to follow my mother's rules for keeping her on the floor, only stroking and cuddling her in my mother's absence. I found the occasions when our budgie escaped from its cage and my mother ran screaming out of our front door whilst I quickly caught it and ran after her, with the bird, still in my hand, to be hilarious and a story well worth repeating. To my shame, I didn't understand the very real anxiety that these things caused her, and I teased her, pretending to take the budgie out of his cage and also enjoyed the retelling of the story, having fun at her expense. She didn't understand the teasing and in retrospect I was able to recognise that these experiences triggered real fear with the resultant flight response.

I have explained how my mother couldn't cook and provided meals of single ingredients such as mushrooms, or broad beans and how this, coupled with her return to work led to me becoming the family cook at quite a young age. My view of cooking is that it brings together a number of senses in collaboration with each other: we utilise our vision to judge that the food looks as it should; our sense of smell to check that our ingredients are fresh, and that the food isn't burning and also that the cooked item smells as it should and our sense of touch to determine consistency. We also use our sense of taste to ensure that it tastes good, before sharing it with others. My mother didn't seem able to use any of these senses, either individually or collaboratively when cooking. She learnt how to cook a Sunday dinner by rote: she bought salt that was in tablet form so that she knew exactly how much to add, and she knew that potatoes needed to boil for twenty minutes so she executed this reliably, but she couldn't mash them as she was unable to judge their texture and couldn't contemplate the possibility of lumps. She had no sense that other vegetables might need less cooking, so all were vigorously boiled to a pulp; meat was always over cooked, and gravy was made without the meat juices, in the way my father had taught her. Sunday dinner always followed the same pattern, with the same tried and tested ingredients and cooking methods. She had a preference for soft, wet food and would love a 'liquidised' version of her roast dinner which had been blended for her grandchildren when they were babies. Her attitude to the Sunday roast puzzled me as, in her rules, the Sunday joint was literally only for the Sunday dinner, so any that was uneaten at dinner time would be thrown away. I tried reasoning and explaining that it could be used in the evening or during the week for sandwiches or other meals, but I was unable to change her attitude or behaviour towards this. I have always disliked waste so I would rescue any leftovers as quickly as possible and turn them in to a stew or a curry, which could be eaten the next day. When I visited as an adult, I always reverted to my role of cook, and whilst my father enjoyed my cooking, my use of different ingredients and dishes was often met with an 'ach a fi' from my mother, or a comment that I cooked 'strange things'. Her eating habits never changed: she remained in her own words 'a fussy eater' and she refused to try any foods which were not already in her limited repertoire. This had always been a source of frustration for me and before recognising the autism link, my attempts at persuading her otherwise caused many arguments. Alongside of this, my mother had some cravings for certain food stuffs, particularly bread and butter, chocolate, cream, and eucalyptus: she would often buy a carton of double cream at work and drink it in her break, and she proudly told everyone that she was a chocoholic. Her liking for strong eucalyptus sweets became an addiction and she would crunch her way through half a pound of them every evening until my father eventually convinced her that they were harmful for her. She broke the habit in typical autistic style and went cold turkey until her compulsions for them passed and she never bought them again.

I grew up not realising that it was unusual to wander the town centre at night, window shopping in preference to browsing the shops in the daytime, and most evenings, I would accompany my mother on one of her regular walks in the town centre, doing precisely this. Having first seen something on one of our jaunts, she was then able to prepare herself for buying it on a future occasion. Again, from an autism perspective, I realised that my mother found the sensory bombardment of daytime browsing and shopping and the requirement for social communication difficult and she recognised that she was able to minimise the difficulties by using these excursions as a coping strategy, enabling her to plan her purchases in advance, and then complete her shopping quickly, whilst avoiding the need to browse at busy times. I would not want to give the impression that I was always the provider and never the recipient of support: my mother was my rock when I returned home pregnant and distraught, following the breakdown of my marriage at the end of 1980; her desire to go walking every evening, accompanied by her objective response to my emotional outpourings was an absolute blessing to me at this time. Like all my emotions, my heartbreak was intense, and I sought release in weeping, external processing and verbal reasoning. My father couldn't bear to listen to my heartbreak so the evening walks with my mother, who just listened and didn't offer any platitudes or solutions was cathartic and healing. Her clear-cut logic challenged my father's view that I must have somehow been responsible for my situation and her defence of me was both rigid and fierce. Something for which I am forever grateful. Whilst I never experienced overt love and affection from my mother, I never doubted her love for me, and this was the time of my life when it was most evident. She was selfless with her time and devotion towards me and allowed me to grieve my loss in my own time, without pressure or expectations. She supported me through the sleepless nights with my new-born daughter and was a loving grandmother whose indulgent generosity could not be faulted.

As mentioned elsewhere, I viewed my mother as a control freak par excellence and in my retrospective assessment of her, this was perhaps the aspect of her character which I needed to understand most in order to bring about any reconciliation. In the earlier chapter, I mentioned that amongst other things, Donna Williams taught me that being autistic in a world that favours the predominant neurotype leads to difficulties with both tolerance and control. My observations were that this was true of my mother, who struggled with both of these character traits. Donna also explained how difficulty in these areas is linked to compulsions and fixations. I have already mentioned in other chapters that my mother had a number of fixations and I've been reminded of many more during the writing of this chapter, but the ones that stand out in my mind for their sheer longevity were: her attachment and fixation on Christmas, Birthday and Valentine cards; her sometimes irrational adherence to The Salvation Army as an organisation, which earned her the nickname from my father of being 'Army barmy'; her rigid need to visit the same hairdresser at the same time every week and her life-long fixation on Coronation Street, and of course her fixation on pre-marital sex. My mother originally watched Coronation Street at my grandmother's house as my uncle rented one, and her fascination with the programme led to us getting our first television set in about 1961. From then on, it is probably accurate to say that she didn't miss an episode. She watched it religiously every Monday and Wednesday evening and then on other evenings as they were added to the schedule, but also, much later on when she could afford a video recorder, she insisted on taping every episode, 'just in case'. I didn't understand her logic at the time and quarrelled with her asking 'in case of what?', but reflecting on it many years later, I realised that her anxiety over missing the programme was so significant that it required a contingency, or a 'what if' plan and she managed this by taking control and recording each episode. This helped her to both manage her anxiety and bring sense into what was otherwise an uncertain reality. It also helped me to understand what I then thought of as her 'Aspie logic'.

More recently, Rudy Simone explains that what she calls 'Aspergirls' can 'take control to a fine art'. She explains how control brings safety and sensory comfort to the anxiety which the female autistic individual experiences when in the unpredictable and unsafe neuro-typical world. She also describes fights over temperature; which television programme to watch; responses to changes to plans and expectations as a 'software crash', which mirrors my mother's melt downs and rages which I've described in more detail elsewhere. This knowledge and insight confirms that my mother's rigid fixations and need for control were not just my mother being difficult but served the purpose of calming her anxiety by managing her environment and expectations.

Whilst my mother's need for sameness and routine provided much needed boundaries and security for me as a baby and a young child, her need to be in control had a negative impact on my life and my relationship with her as I sought to develop independence. I explained in Chapter 6, how the effects of her obsession with sex affected me and our family, but her need to stick rigidly to her timings and routines was another area of stress and contention for me. Mealtimes had to be at certain fixed time throughout her life so that dinner was at 12 pm (even on Christmas day), and tea, (when she was working) was as soon as she got home. The routine changed after her retirement to lunch at 12 pm, tea at 5 pm, followed by a supper at 9 pm. As I have already mentioned, I took over the cooking of the evening meal for the family, from quite a young age. I enjoyed cooking, although I did once set the chip pan on fire which fortunately my father was able to deal with before it caused any damage, but on reflection, my mother's rigid mealtime routines caused me a great deal of stress. For most of her working life, the supermarket where she worked closed at 5. 30 pm (8 pm on a Friday) after which there would then be a period of cashing up. The length of time this would take varied, depending on the accuracy of the takings in the tills. My mother prided herself in the accuracy of her till, but there were occasions when she would be delayed by her manager's mathematical inaccuracies which then required a recount. My mother didn't drive, being far too anxious, although she had an exceptional knowledge of the Highway Code and was an excellent back seat driver, so my father always collected her from work arriving in the pre-arranged waiting place prior to the closing time of 5.30 pm, knowing that he would suffer my mother's wrath, should she be allowed to leave early, which of course she never did. The speed of the cashing up process would determine the time that they arrived home, but my mother's rigidly exacting standards required the meal, accompanied by a slice of bread and butter and a cup of tea, to be on the table, ready for her at the precise minute that she walked through the front door. I learnt cooking skills and techniques for ensuring this but making the tea at the precise moment was particularly challenging as her sensitive taste buds couldn't tolerate anything but a freshly brewed cup and she was unable to wait if there was a delay. To overcome this, I would boil the kettle shortly after my father had left the house to collect her and then I would wait in the front room to watch for their arrival. As soon as I saw my father's van come down our road, I would then rush into the kitchen to quickly re-boil the already hot kettle so that I could 'wet the tea' as they say in Wales, and put the meals on the table, at the exact moment that my parents walked through the door. My mother was unable to tolerate the wait if I misjudged the timing and her irritability at this was best avoided if possible. I never remember her thanking me for the meal, and I never expected her gratitude: it was what it was, and I did what I did. I experienced intense grief after my father died, and when this was followed in a relatively short period by the death of my mother and then my sister, I suffered a reactive depression for which I received counselling. During the counselling process I was led to see how unusual, unreasonable, and stressful this arrangement was for me as a child. My counsellor, unlike me, seemed to think that it was potentially abusive, but I disagreed with this. It was what it was, and I've never felt any sense of wrong relating to it. I cooked because I wanted to, out of love for my parents and I enjoyed cooking, as I still do. It's a gift I give to those who I love and like all gifts, I don't expect anything in return for it. That it became an expected part of my mother's routine was an unfortunate knock-on effect from that but as an adult I recognised that my mother's need for routine and control was part of how she maintained her inner calm and equilibrium. I don't think that my mother took me for granted but she was unable to show her gratitude and respond differently.

I am aware that my assessment of my mother may have focused significantly on her sensory differences. These are now at long last, recognised in the DSM V criteria as being 'companions' of autism, albeit under the banner of 'restricted, repetitive patterns of behaviour, interests, or activities'. My personal view is that this welcome beginning does not go far enough in improving diagnosis or our understanding of autism. I am firmly convinced that the sensory environment plays a significant part in the presentation of autism, a view which is supported by the simple equation: autism + environment = outcome, put forward by Dr Luke Beardon, in Asperger Syndrome in Adults (2017). It is logical to me that as all information is received through our senses, then the environment, which is made up of sensory stimuli must be central to the processing of all information. Taking this into account, I take the view that sensory perception, and differences in sensory processing are therefore at the heart of an individual's presentation of autism: they affect the degree and intensity of experience and response, or what Beardon calls 'outcome', so when the environment is suitable for autistic people, then the outcome is favourable and vice versa. As sensory perception is at the heart of processing the environment, it must then of necessity play a significant role in the outcome. For this reason, I've chosen to focus significant part of my recorded unofficial 'assessment' of my mother, on her sensory differences. The recognition of the role of differences in sensory perception as being central to the individual presentation of autism is still however a relatively new concept and its significance is unfortunately not always recognised by diagnosticians or support practitioners.

Until relatively recently, autism was viewed as a Communication Disorder and deficits in communication (now linked with social interaction), are still given precedence in the DSM V diagnostic criteria, followed by 'restricted, repetitive patterns of behaviour, interests, or activities', which now include differences in sensory input and perception. Given their place in the diagnostic criteria, it was appropriate for exploration of my mother's autism to include both communication and social interaction.

My mother struggled to communicate effectively: she was often seemingly mute, particularly outside of the home, or excessively verbose, when she talked incessantly at great speed in a one-sided conversation. It was difficult to have a conversation with her which was between these two extremes; she rarely had topics of conversation, although she did talk about people who she knew, and she didn't engage in small talk. She was significantly indiscrete, to the point of rudeness at times and she frequently overshared information, causing others to be embarrassed. She retained her childhood vocabulary and phrases throughout her life, particularly those to do with bodily parts and functions such as constipation, which was always referred to as being 'stiff', and she had no sense of appropriate language registers. She often amused us with her malapropisms, and on one occasion she tried to impress us by using the word 'masticate' which she mistakenly replaced with 'masturbate'. She also replaced 'chit chatting' with 'twit twatting', to repeat just two. She had certain trigger words that offended her, and which were guaranteed to get a reaction: 'fart' was one example and her grandchildren used to purposely tease her with this, just to get a reaction and to hear her say 'Oh I hate that word' in her strong Welsh accent. She had little awareness or skill in turn taking so would either not join in conversations or she would interrupt inappropriately or talk over others. Listening was a skill which eluded her.

I have already mentioned strategies which my mother used effectively to avoid unwanted conversations and how she attempted to use scripts to prepare for unavoidable social interactions, sometimes with more success than others. One of my earliest memories relates to when, at about eighteen months or two years old, I badly scalded my left hand and arm. I don't remember the accident, but I do remember the smell of the medicated gauze that was used as a dressing and I also remember being in my mother's arms when she distracted me by drawing my attention to the flickering of the gas fire in the doctor's surgery, whilst he lanced the very large blisters that I had on my wrist and forearm. I also remember that I was aware of my mother practising a script prior to this appointment, which she repeatedly rehearsed under her breath, muttering to herself in the waiting room. This continued to be part of her routine preparation for any planned meeting with professionals such as doctors, shop assistants and hairdressers, throughout her life and I have memories of her bursting into tears when the conversation took an unexpected turn from her script. These social scripts are now recognised as effective strategies which help autistic people manage the uncertainty of common interactions and are often rehearsed in 'what if' scenarios with autistic people. In retrospect, when focusing my attention on my understanding and 'assessing' of my mother, I realised that this was also a strategy which she used to manage her anxiety and assist her communication. Similarly, my mother would verbally repeat past conversations, muttering under her breath, as part of her retrospective understanding and processing of them. I now of course also recognise this as a coping strategy for processing and understanding.

My mother was a loner for most of her life but in her later years talked about her 'friends' and I wondered who these were as my observations were that she had no close reciprocal relationships with anyone other than my father, and that she probably had a different concept of friendship to most people. She attended a slimming club for about twenty years and in the last five years of her life she got to know two women there who she considered to be her friends. My observations were that she had no contact with them, other than at the weekly meetings but they did visit her occasionally when her deteriorating health prevented her continued attendance. I believe that my mother appreciated this although she never expressed her appreciation and often complained about the disruptive effect they had on her routine, but she certainly did not initiate any meetings outside of the slimming club environment. Similarly, she talked about women at the Army as her friends, particularly one who sat next to her in the Sunday meetings. This 'friendship' also did not extend to any contact other than that on the Sunday evening.

I have not mentioned my mother's emotional outbursts and seeming lack of emotional regulation in this chapter, believing that I have already provided a sufficient description of these in earlier chapters. It is sufficient to say here that my mother had many triggers for her outbursts and meltdowns, which were often extreme, but on reflection, I think that the previously mentioned equation of autism + environment = outcome explains these, together with her sense and fear of a loss of control which was central to all. Life in a world which catered predominantly for the majority neurotype was challenging for her, and she struggled most, and possibly all of the time to maintain emotional stability.

And then there was empathy!

People often confuse empathy with sympathy. Whilst the two are similar, there is a difference: empathy is the ability to understand and share the feelings of another; to put oneself in their situation and to feel what they feel. Sympathy on the other hand is to feel pity for someone else. Autistic people are traditionally considered to lack empathy, although this view is quite rightly criticised and challenged. This inaccurate view has arisen out of one of the psychological theories put forward by predominant neurotype academics who view autism as observable behaviour which is found to be lacking when measured against the neurotypical norm. This theory posits the view that autistic people lack a Theory of Mind which in turn leads to a lack of empathy.

Donna Williams in Autism, An Inside-Out Approach (1996) whilst acknowledging that autistic people can struggle to process and understand others' intentions during social interactions also says that if we listen to autistic people, we find that such difficulties are reciprocal. She concludes that a mutual misunderstanding between the autistic and dominant neurotype is at the heart of the empathy issue, a view which has more recently been taken up by Damien Milton in what he terms The Double Empathy Theory. This was certainly the case for my mother: empathy is a two-way street and whilst my mother was seemingly unable to demonstrate empathy it seemed to me that she wasn't afforded any either. Later, after learning about the 'double empathy problem' (DEP), I realised that I had been blinded by the closeness of our relationship, and that this, coupled with my learned automatic responses had resulted in me making few attempts to empathise with my mother's lived experience. A short time before my father died, my late sister chastised my mother, telling her that the physical and emotional demands which she was placing on my father would kill him. My mother, who loved my father deeply and who literally wasn't able to live without him, responded with 'well, he's three and a half years older than me so he's bound to die before me'. As shocking as that statement was, by this time, my recognition that my mother was autistic, and my understanding of the DEP enabled me to respond empathetically.

My father died a few months later without understanding my mother's autism, and my mother was bereft. They were the opposite sides of the same coin. Perhaps both were autistic!

CHAPTER 9

Acceptance and reconciliation

I often talked to my father about what he termed my mother's 'strange behaviours' and he took the view that they came about because of her upbringing: most particularly because she had been brought up by two old fashioned and narrow-minded Welsh women; one of whom was a spinster who had either a learning difficulty or a mental illness, the other (my grandmother), he described as rigidly narrow minded and dogmatic in her beliefs. He argued that this narrow female dominated upbringing had resulted in my mother's 'peculiar ways'. I found this reasoning difficult to accept for several reasons. Firstly, it wasn't accurate: my grandfather had been involved in my mother's upbringing for the first fifteen years of her life and whilst I found it feasible that he might, given his reportedly mild nature and the gender roles and expectations of the time, have allowed my grandmother to have full control over nurturing their children, I couldn't accept that living in the cramped conditions of the family home, would have enabled him to be totally excluded from exerting some influence. Then, my father swept my mother off her feet, when she was only seventeen years old and they remained together for over sixty years, so I argued that he would have had a significantly greater influence over her than either my grandmother or Aunty Jenny. My perception and memories of Aunty Jenny and my grandmother also didn't fit with his explanation: I was only eleven when my grandmother died but we had a close relationship and my memories of her are clear. Whilst I appreciate that these may have been rose tinted and altered over time, my late sister and my mother's brother, both also remembered a strong formidable woman who was old fashioned, but not more so than other Welsh women of her generation. We remembered a woman who had faced life's difficulties, including a scandal involving her son, with courage and fortitude whilst maintaining her pride in her family. I recalled her determination and support when she escorted my mother's return to my father on the one occasion early in their marriage when my mother had left the family home, and my interpretation of this was one, of a mother who was encouraging her daughter to be a responsible and an independent adult, who faced up to her responsibilities, and not one who encouraged 'strange behaviour' or dependency. Aunty Jenny, on the other hand was a nervous and gentle soul, who I knew well as she was an important part of my life until I was twenty-two. I found it inconceivable that this quietly subservient and servile woman could exert any influence over anyone, let alone my mother. I argued that there must be another reason for my mother's rigid thinking and beliefs, but my father refused to see my point of view and I many times parroted the argument that 'behaviour which is learnt can be unlearnt', in an attempt to convince my father that my mother's so called 'strange behaviours' were part of who she was, and that numerous opportunities for her to unlearn them or learn new ones had not brought about any change. This argument always fell on deaf ears however and my father's rigid thinking prevailed. It was also impossible for my father to recognise that many of his behaviours triggered my mother's responses. He took great pleasure in being mischievous throughout his life and whilst my mother continually reminded him that she 'didn't have a sense of humour', he was unable to stop himself from baiting her with humorous taunts. This 'poking the sleeping bear' as my husband described it was the cause of significant friction and arguments and their relationship continued its volatile path without him acknowledging his role in it, or her autism , until he died in 2009. My Damascene experience was however life changing.

I first took part in delivering Autism Awareness training in 1995 and it was exciting as extending knowledge of autism into the public domain was quite new. Autism awareness has since become a global initiative so that we now celebrate Autism Awareness Week, at the beginning of April every year. The National Autistic Society (NAS) describes this event on their website as: *"Aiming to draw attention to the 700,000 people living with autism in the UK both to educate those unaware of the condition, and to help make the world friendlier to those who are affected by it."* The NAS events page then goes on to explain how it will promote work or school-based initiatives, and how virtual events will raise money for autistic people in the UK. Elsewhere, across the world, people are encouraged to wear blue on the 2nd of April, and are asked to unite in support of autism charities. A quick internet search will give results of further well-meaning descriptions of the month of April as being an opportunity to raise money for Autism charities, through a widespread campaign which includes sponsored events across the globe. It is suggested that this will 'bring more prominence to the issues that people living with Autism face'. A slightly more detailed internet search will unearth lists of these 'initiatives', whilst a significantly more detailed search will uncover why autistic people dislike the concept of autism awareness, identifying the need to move from awareness to understanding and then to acceptance and action, alongside of extending the concept of autism awareness beyond one day or month of the year. These more detailed searches will also find autistic people's objections to the 'lighting the world blue' initiative, arguing that this campaign supports and promotes negative stereotypes of autism. These differences in thinking and opinions are worth exploring as they highlight the challenges and the gulf in perspective between the dominant neurotype's view of autistic people's needs and autistic people's articulation of them.

In 2004, when I began my journey of understanding my mother as an autistic person, I had studied autism at undergraduate and Master's degree level and I had also learnt from autistic people for many years, so it would not have been arrogant for me to consider myself as having a high level of autism awareness and understanding. In my professional life, I was accepting of people's autism, strongly advocating a social model approach to support, which would always seek to prioritise changing the environment, rather than the autistic person. My experience of advocacy took me deeper in my thinking and led me down a path which I was eager to follow: a path to true autism acceptance. The Welsh autistic man I was advocating for believed that other's attitudes, behaviour and responses towards him would change if they became aware of his autism, but this was not his, or my experience. There was no change in attitudes towards him, on the contrary, he was often accused of using his autism as an excuse for what others saw as his 'challenging behaviour'. At this time, I was already questioning why many years of autism awareness training and conferences had little practical impact on the lived experience of autistic people, and the unique position of advocate, which required me to identify with the autistic person and put myself firmly in their shoes, caused me to reflect on the autism experience on a more personal level, further challenging and deepening my thinking. Through listening to autistic people, I learned that autism awareness as an entity, perpetuates negative stereotypes because it presents autism as being something other than 'normal'; a problem that needs to be solved. It imparts knowledge of a 'disorder' or a 'condition' where words and phrases such as communication impairment; autistic traits; difficulties; challenges; issues, and lack of empathy are used to convey understanding of this state of being, which is portrayed as abnormal. Autism awareness had mistakenly and incorrectly presented the autism spectrum as linear, demonstrating the stereotypical extremes, with non-verbal, 'flapping' people who are unable to take care of themselves at one end, and the stereotypical IT nerd, or Maths genius at the other. Alongside of this it had encouraged the use of functioning labels, focusing on the deficits of the 'low functioning' or the 'less able', whilst denying their strengths and focusing on the abilities of the 'high functioning', whilst being blind to the challenges, difficulties and effort which they experienced. An awareness of lack of emotions and empathy featured prominently, with no recognition of neurotypical responsibilities in this area and females were excluded from the picture, allowing, or even encouraging the male stereotype of autism to dominate. Stereotypical views of autism are also perpetuated in the inclusion of so called 'autistic strengths', such as a need for routine; attention to detail; perseverance, or savant skills, and autistic people often feel that they are limited by these stereotypical characteristics which often morph into myths. Employment support has been directed at playing to these perceived or expected strengths thus further perpetuating these myths, and autistic people have been directed into low-aspirational, boring, repetitive jobs on the understanding that their need for routine, or perseverance correlates with enjoyment and fulfilment, regardless of their qualifications, aspirations and personal goals. When viewed from this perspective, it is easy to see why autistic people feel that decades of autism awareness have failed them.

Similarly, the 'light it up blue' autism awareness campaign is disliked by autistic people who understand the negative connotations associated with this and who challenge the ethical stance of the organisations who promote it. Semiotics, which is the academic study into how signs and symbols create meaning can help us understand this. It teaches us that words, both written or spoken, are symbols or signs used to communicate and that there are two relatively basic levels of meaning: denotation and connotation, which all signs and symbols convey. Simply explained, denotation is the basic, or literal meaning of the sign, whilst connotation refers to a more subtle, cultural, and emotional meaning which is signified by that sign. Denotations are objective, or neutral, whilst connotations can be positive or negative depending on the cultural or emotional connections they have. Semiotics also teaches that the connotation of the chosen sign can be purposeful or accidental and that their cultural and emotional significance is ingrained in native users of a language.

Colours are signs which have connotations, so in Western culture, red for example signifies hot, sexy and danger whilst blue signifies cold, maleness, and low mood. Connotations are powerful and relied on heavily by the advertising industry as a means of subtly and successfully influencing the potential market for a product, with large companies investing heavily to ensure that their advertising uses the most effective connotations to reach their target audience and achieve their desired effect. Some autistic people therefore argue that it is inconceivable that the large organisation behind the promotion of the 'light it up blue' campaign for autism awareness would be unaware of the negative connotations and stereotypes which their choice of colour would convey, an opinion which is supported by Angela Geiger, the founder of the organisation openly stating that their choice of a blue light was influenced by the dominance of male autism diagnoses over female. Autistic people also argue that the campaign itself, in using these negative connotations under the banner of building autism awareness, is harmful and promotes and reinforces negative stereotypes with the primary aim of fundraising, the main beneficiary of which being the organisation itself: an organisation whose driving principle is to eradicate autism from society. When these views are listened to, it is easy to see why autism awareness has failed autistic people.

In 2004, I was embarking on my own journey to understanding why decades of autism awareness and academic teaching had been ineffective in improving attitudes and professional practices, as well as removing the discrimination which autistic people were experiencing. Listening to autistic people taught me that autism awareness, however well-presented was a passive act of receiving knowledge, which on its own did nothing to effect change, and that change could only be achieved through moving on from awareness to understanding and then acceptance. Acceptance is defined as the "general agreement that something is satisfactory or right, or that someone should be included in a group": something which requires positive action on the part of a recipient. If this is correct, then true acceptance of autism and autistic people as equal contributors in society places a responsibility on the dominant neurotype to not only be aware of autism, but to engage in a cognitive shift towards a full understanding of what it is to be autistic. This means that those who share the dominant neurology must put in time and effort to listen to autistic people and learn from them and most importantly accept them as they are. This must then be followed by focused intentional action to adapt and change unconscious and ingrained ways of thinking and behaving so that autistic people can be fully included.

Moving from awareness to acceptance of my mother as autistic, was not an easy or straightforward journey as I had many deeply held negative thoughts and beliefs concerning her which needed confronting and exorcising. I had long been familiar with Philip Larkin's poem, This Be The Verse, which succinctly describes the negative impact that parenting has on subsequent generations and I was aware of how certain aspects of my upbringing, particularly my father's criticism, had impacted on me. I am a ruminator and I had long since exhausted my ruminations over this and many years before had reached a point of forgiveness on the basis that both of my parents did the best parenting that they could with the tools that were available to them, and they had both done it well. I loved both of my parents and held no resentment towards them, but I was ashamed to say that I didn't like my mother.

Anyone who knows me well, especially professionally, will know that I love language and that I have always been an advocate of inclusive language. In 2006 I wrote in The Autism Spectrum and Further Education that *'language is an extremely powerful tool which has the ability to change how people think'*, and that *'our choice of words influences our perceptions of people and things'*. As indicated in earlier chapters, I used negative words when I thought and spoke of my mother and these words were both influenced by, and in turn influenced my thoughts of her. Professionally, I always practiced, taught, and encouraged the use of positive, inclusive language for autism, so I reverted to my professional, rather than my familial role, when undertaking an unofficial, non-clinical autism assessment of mother. All assessment has to come from a position of understanding: firstly, of understanding autism generally and then understanding how autism presents itself for that specific individual. My understanding of my mother altered dramatically through exploring her autism as it not only confirmed what I had already suspected but it revealed more of her autism than I had previously seen. My understanding of her was also significantly improved through consciously changing the language which I used about her. Examples of words I changed were: selfish became focused on her needs; stubbornness became perseverance; difficult became stressed or anxious; liar was eliminated in preference for a different perception to mine, aggression became defensiveness, and obsessed became fascinated or fixated. Instead of seeing her as 'difficult', I saw her as struggling to cope in an environment that clashed with her neurological make up and her 'emotional outbursts' and 'rages' became autistic melt downs caused by emotional or sensory overload. I was able to see that her need for control and routine were coping strategies for the anxiety which she experienced in an uncertain and unpredictable world and with that understanding came patience. Some of this happened instantly but I recognise that it took time to reach a full understanding and I am continuing to process and develop this, eight years after her death. Some may see this as the rewriting of history but for me, as a self-confessed ruminator, this retrospective processing is an essential part of achieving full understanding of her and my relationship with her.

Intellectual acceptance of my mother's autism was easy as I hold no negative views on the subject, choosing to view autism as one of the whole range of diverse neurological types which we call normal. Emotional and practical acceptance was however more difficult as it required action. It required me to put aside my long-held inaccuracies, perceptions and emotional hurts and to re-evaluate and own some preconceived notions and prejudices about autism which I didn't recognise I had. I struggled with reconciling the aspects of my mother's character and personality which I disliked, such as her anger, and it took some time to reconcile myself with the understanding that whilst I still do not know the reasons for her anger and aggression, these were not caused by her autism, but were an autistic response and defence to her experience. I was then able to look at triggers for her anger so that I could avoid or minimise these in my interactions with her. This wasn't easy as old habits are difficult to break and I wasn't always successful.

With acceptance came the realisation that I shouldn't attempt to change my mother; something which I had been guilty of throughout my life, but which I would challenge in my professional life. This brought a sense of freedom and release both emotionally and practically as the change in my behaviour effected in a change in the relationship with my mother.

In many ways, my realisation of my mother's autism came too late as I became aware that she had dementia in 2007 and she was diagnosed with Alzheimer's in 2009, shortly after the death of my father, and her withdrawal into her own world was rapid. With more time, I might have been able to understand her better and talk to her about her experience and helped her to reduce her anxiety, but I doubt if she would have been receptive to this, and I suspect that she would have been resistant, even when younger.

The reconciliation was short, but we were closer in the four years before her death that we had been before, and I understood her better. I believe that loved ones live on in our memories of them and my family remembers my mother as she was, with great affection and humour. Being the ruminator that I am, the analysis, the reconciliation and the understanding continues.

CHAPTER 10

Am I pretending?

My Heart Leaps Up
My heart leaps up when I behold
A rainbow in the sky:
So was it when my life began;
So is it now I am a man;
So be it when I shall grow old,
Or let me die!
The Child is father of the Man;
And I could wish my days to be
Bound each to each by natural piety.
(William Wordsworth 1807)

I used to attend, and sometimes speak at conferences but that was before I realised that they weren't essential to either my professional or personal development. My husband describes me as having no ego, so I gain no satisfaction from being invited to speak and I've been fortunate that I've had no need to access the networking opportunities which I'm told conferences offer. Managing the budget of a not-for-profit organisation made it difficult to justify incurring a company loss of income plus a sometimes-large expenditure, whilst I attended an event which I felt didn't offer value for money and took up time which should have been spent doing the work I loved: supporting autistic students. Whilst I enjoy learning, especially from autistic people, I found that I preferred the more intimate environment of talks, or training sessions delivered by autistic individuals, as they were significantly more informative and rewarding. I could be accused of making excuses when the reality is that I found conferences expensive, stressful and exhausting, but my dislike of conferences stemmed from all of these things. I found it difficult to tolerate neuro-typical speakers who sometimes entertained the audience by appropriating autistic anecdotes to their own advantage; I was critical of those speakers who would turn up, literally just in time to deliver their talk and then leave immediately afterwards, without attempting to engage with their audience; I can also be quite pedantic about inclusive language, believing that conferences should be at the heart of promoting good practice in this area and am frustrated if they fail to do that, and I expect to come away with new ideas which challenge and develop my existing knowledge and thinking, even if those ideas are opposed to mine. I was always disappointed if my perhaps exacting requirements for a good conference were not met, and I would feel some irrational sense of personal responsibility or blame for that. I used to look forward to, but also dreaded the buffet table as I had to fight my desire to load my plate with a little of everything whilst worrying that others might think me greedy. I would scan other delegate's plates surreptitiously so that I could judge the right amount of food to put on mine, thinking that if I took too little, I could always go back for more in the hope that no one would notice that I was queuing for the second time. Having loaded my plate, I then had to somehow find a way to eat the longed-for morsels, whilst balancing my plate in one hand and a cup and saucer in the other. I watched and copied other people and would try to find somewhere to put my drink so that one hand was free to convey the food to my mouth whilst I would simultaneously frantically scan the room, looking for anyone I knew, whilst also reading people's body language to see if there was anyone who, like me was on their own, perhaps also looking for someone to talk to. I could guarantee that someone would engage me in conversation just at the moment that I'd taken a bite from my favourite egg, or prawn mayonnaise sandwich and from then on, any conversation would be peppered with worries about whether I was spitting crumbs at them; had mayonnaise running down my chin; when was a suitable time to put food in my mouth, or whether my breath smelled of the recently eaten egg or prawn mayonnaise which I'm very partial to. Having successfully navigated those obstacles, I would realise that I could no longer remember the name of the person who I was talking to and as I didn't have my reading glasses on and didn't have a free hand to retrieve them from my bag, I couldn't be rescued by subtly reading the name badge that they were wearing. In many ways it was easier when I was a speaker as I have no difficulty speaking in public and people would at least know who I was and would sometimes want to speak to me and ask me relatively predictable questions during the break times. Often at these times, people would ask how and why I became interested in working in the field of autism and for many years I shrugged my shoulders and told them that it was something that I just seemed to be good at: a kind of 'innate' ability, inaccurately implying that I just drifted into it, when it was in reality a conscious decision. After 2004, I would simply tell people that it was because my mother was autistic and say that this had provided the springboard for my interest and had taught me the required skills. This predictably triggered a conversation about my mother, which was always easy to engage in.

In 2014, Spectrum First organised a Women and Autism conference where I spoke in public about my mother for the first time. The conference was organised with the intention of being both financially and environmentally accessible to autistic people and Wenn Lawson, who was just embarking on the process of transitioning was the keynote speaker. Dr Richard Smith talked about diagnosing girls; Penny Andrews talked about her experience as a University student, and I spoke about my life with an autistic mother. I loved being in the company of so many autistic people, even though they were mostly women, and for the first time in a conference enjoyed the lunch break as there was lots of space with circular tables to sit at. Whilst queuing for the buffet, the woman behind me in the queue told me how much she had enjoyed my talk and said to me *'and what about you Christine? Are you autistic or have you pretended for so long that you don't know?'* Over the years, many autistic people have told me that they suspect that I am autistic or that I have many 'autistic traits', so it wasn't unusual for me to be asked this but this woman's additional comment of *'or have you pretended for so long that you don't know?'* surprised and challenged my thinking in a way which hadn't happened previously. I ruminated over this conversation in verbatim, for some time and I have returned to it frequently in the intervening years. Autistic people continue to ask me if I'm autistic or say things like *'to be frank, I think you're also autistic'* or *'why don't you go and get diagnosed?'* and I have considered this, but I have come to the realisation that I have no need for confirmation either way. This is perhaps a bit perverse for someone who advocates the positive aspects of labelling, being convinced that the autism label is preferable to the alternative labels that are often attached to undiagnosed autistic people and who, if labelled would wear the autism label with pride. I have reasoned that if I was still a teenager or still in Higher Education or some other employment, then a diagnosis might be of significant benefit to me, but those periods have long passed, and they are not motivations for me. A diagnosis wouldn't potentially open any doors at this stage in my life; I don't need support, and a diagnosis (if that was to be made) would no longer be of professional benefit to me. Most importantly, I don't have any questions which a diagnosis would answer or provide explanations for what I know and feel about myself, and it wouldn't change how those who love me feel about me. I don't consider autism as a superior or an inferior neurological state of being, so I have nothing to prove. I am loved as I am, for who I am and that for me, at this point in time is sufficient.

Cataloguing my journey to understanding my mother's autism has required me to reveal much about myself and my own neurology in the earlier chapters of this book. As an over sharer, I have few, if any secrets, and having a tendency towards truthfulness I have endeavoured to be honest and open about myself throughout, but whilst I feel that I have already disclosed significant information about me, I am aware that the question posed to me in 2014 remains unanswered. If I am to truly honour autism and autistic mothers, then I recognise that I am required to address this question: what about me? Am I so used to pretending that I don't know whether I am autistic or not? Have I been masking and pretending for so long that it is now impossible for me to know who is the real me? The simple answer to the question is 'yes', but I acknowledge this simple answer as being insufficient to fulfil my purpose in writing this book. There is a need for further exploration, but I am unable to provide a definitive answer: I leave that, if needed, for others to decide as I am genuinely content either way.

I always thought that the phrase 'the child is father to the man' was coined by Freud because it seemed to be the type of statement he would make, but I recently discovered that it was William Wordsworth who in 1807 used this phrase in his poem My Heart Leaps up, (also called The Rainbow), which I've quoted at the beginning of this chapter. I wish that Wordsworth had talked about women and mothers, but he was after all writing from the experience of being male, and I no longer rail against the sexism of early nineteenth century writers, preferring to direct my efforts to challenging current struggles for women's rights and equality. In this poem, Wordsworth talks about his childhood pleasure and wonder in nature, and he encourages the reader to carry these pleasures with them into old age. This poem, or more specifically the sentence *"the child is father to the man"*, resonates with my own life: my childhood may not have been as idyllic and wonderous as that which was Wordsworth's experience, but my childhood experiences planted the seeds of a lifelong passion which, despite at times bringing me to my knees with genuine grief and helplessness for the tragic and devastating experiences of others, has also filled me with both wonder and joy, which I have taken with me into adulthood.

When the unknown woman asked me during the conference if I had *'pretended for so long that I didn't know'*, it immediately reminded me of Leanne Holliday Willey, who wrote Pretending to Be Normal, which I read when it was first published in 1999. I had at the time recognised some similarities: I've been told that I am blunt and outspoken and to my horror, in 1997, when I studied on a Higher Access Course prior to attending University, I had been told that others had found me intimidating. I had ruminated over this and talked about it at length with my husband and I had finally attributed this quality to my Welsh choice of vocabulary, accent and use of language and emphasis. Like Willey, I have a love of language and linguistics, and had studied the subject, so I was aware of language registers, and I used this awareness to address my speech by working to change my perhaps formal register to one that was more consultative and casual, although I am still aware that I sometimes come across as dogmatic. After 2014, I started to question if this was pretending, or was it just what everyone does? My love of language use has at times led to me being called pedantic or literal: I recoil when people use the wrong negative prefix for example: 'unorganised' instead of 'disorganised'; or 'uninterested' when it should be 'disinterested' and I find it difficult to tolerate the misuse of the apostrophe. The inaccurate use of the words 'I' or 'myself', when it should be 'me' is particularly irritating for me. These may seem relatively minor details, but they are painful for me, and I have to rein in my compulsions to correct them. Certain phrases can also trigger an immediate emotional response such as: 'what you want to do is…..' which is guaranteed to trigger an immediate anger which I have learnt to control and suppress and the phrase 'take your seats', often used in a congregational setting is also guaranteed to trigger a desire to correct or respond argumentatively. I also dislike intensely, the current usage of the phrase 'reached out' as for me it verges on being a euphemism. I am aware that others might have similar reactions, but I suspect that the intensity of mine is greater and again, I have learnt to control and suppress my responses, if not my thoughts. Are these examples of pretending? Similarly to Willey, I work hard at fitting in and worry and ruminate over the impact of my words and actions on others: I worry that I may have been misunderstood; or that I may have caused offence, or that I have made myself look foolish. I acknowledge that not everyone does this and those who do, may not do it as intensely or persistently as I do. No one, apart from my husband knows the excruciating extent of my worries and ruminations as I'm well practiced in hiding them. Is this also pretending? I have always had an intense dislike for social organisations so given the choice, I refused to be a Brownie or a Girl Guide, preferring to be the only girl in an otherwise all male friendship group, and brass band. I loved choral singing where I was part of a group with a clearly defined purpose and role and I could sight-read almost anything, and I loved performing with a scripted part in plays and musicals but found ways to avoid taking part in other organised group activities, unless accompanied by my one friend or boyfriend. I now question if this avoidance, which I generally defended by disparaging the group or activity, was also a form of pretending. I wear my emotions on my sleeve but learnt to conceal my temper and my anxiety to the point where they became invisible. Like my mother, I have a need to control but unlike my mother, I have no desire to control others, and have directed that control so successfully towards my unwanted character traits that I have virtually extinguished temper and anxiety's existence, fearing the consequences that a loss of control brings. This pretence, if it is pretence, has come at great cost to my health, as this level of self-control and the suppression and internalisation of anxiety has been at least partly responsible for forty years of suffering with ulcerative colitis and other chronic inflammatory illnesses.

Autistic pretence at being 'normal' has become recognised in recent years, particularly in relation to autistic women, with terms like camouflaging and masking being introduced to explain this phenomenon, but as always, experience precedes research so there are currently few academic explanations or validations of this lived experience. My own knowledge gained through studying communication raises questions: Many years ago, I learnt that everyone adapts their communication and behaviour to a greater or lesser degree to conform to the cultural expectations of their environment, but I have no doubt that the degree of masking required of autistic people is significantly greater than that of the general population. Most people conform to cultural expectations, but masking involves a degree of pretence or a false representation of that person, which is far more significant than covering up or modifying some behaviours. It requires the person to deny a part of themselves and to pretend to be someone other than who they are in order to fit into their host culture. This raises questions about the cultural status of autism which will no doubt be the subject of further academic study and answered by people other than me. Willey (2015) refers to having a bi-cultural Asperger Syndrome and neuro-typical identity, which she moves between, according to her situation, circumstances, and her need for pretence. I identify with this as since leaving Wales, I have always felt a stranger in a foreign land and have previously attributed this to my Welshness, questioning why not all Welsh 'exiles' share my experience, and wondering if there could be another dimension to my sense of difference. This difference extends to many areas of my life, and I am aware of having to 'fake it to make it' in many situations where I consider it worthwhile for me to do so. If I am unable to fake it, then I find ways around it, for example:

I have an irrational panic response when in libraries and bookshops, which triggers a breakdown in visual processing followed by the flight or fight response. When I was a student, university study relied on accessing the library, so my husband, who loves books, would support me with this by getting the books from the library for me, or I would buy the books I needed and ask someone else to photocopy journal papers for me. Is all of this pretending to be normal?

There are other areas which I could explore to a deeper extent than this chapter allows, but it is not my intention to provide a personal diagnostic check list of my character traits and behaviours, believing that I have indicated many in earlier chapters, but empathy is an area which I cannot ignore as I suffer from an excess of it. I first identified this at the age of twelve, when my father had an appendectomy, although I didn't know that it was excess empathy at the time. His insistence on showing me his wound when I visited him in hospital caused me physical pain around the area of my own appendix which I only knew to describe as sympathy pains. My experience as an adult is that I am overly sensitive to other's emotions and responses, as well as physical experiences, which can (especially when combined with my tendency to rumination and a possession of an unusual memory), be both physically and mentally debilitating. I have found this trait useful professionally but unhelpful socially: it helps me to understand and identify with the people who I support and as a trainer, enables me to pick up on confusion or conflicting thoughts and reactions in the audience very easily, but it is accompanied by a great social and emotional cost when I am oversensitive to potentially negative reactions. I have learnt to live with this as I embrace its benefits, whilst trying to ignore its detriments, but it is still difficult sometimes.

I am familiar with the concept of residual autism and the debate which resulted in its removal from the DSM criteria in 1987. I had thought that the suggestion that people could recover from autism was outdated and harmful, arising out of the pathologising of autism, which I find dehumanising and discriminatory, and I had hoped the term was extinct. I was disappointed and dismayed to read that Willey (2015) says that Tony Attwood, (someone who is held in high esteem for his expertise in the field of autism) uses this term, describing her as *'a woman with residual Asperger Syndrome'*. She explains that this label is attributed to her because she has 'reconfigured *much of [her] thinking and many of [her] behaviours to fit within society's norms'*. She continues to say that living with *'one foot in neuro-typical land and one foot in Aspie land'* is stressful and that she is happiest when in *'Aspie land'*. I am saddened by this as it exemplifies the reality of autistic people's experience of living in a culture which continues to put the onus on them to change and accommodate, whilst excusing the dominant neurotypical culture from any responsibility for including and embracing them. I rail against this and will always challenge it, but this presents a dilemma for me, perhaps similar to that of Willey's where I have to live in a society which requires me to move between two camps: one of the idealist, who wants autistic utopia, where everyone can be themselves, and the other of the realist who has to accept and adapt to the neurotypical reality. Applying this to the question of this chapter: 'what about me?', causes me to question if I would be given the label of residual autistic. As the autism diagnostic criteria are founded within a pathologised, medical model of autism, and as most diagnostic practitioners comply with this medical model, I suspect that could be a realistic but not ideal possibility which would not sit comfortably with me.

Whilst it is not my intention to indulge in the nature nurture debate in relation to the causation of autism, it would be impossible for me to complete this chapter without addressing this concept in the context of autism diagnosis, as I believe that my background, both in terms of upbringing and knowledge of autism would impact significantly on any potential diagnosis. This nature versus nurture debate is one of the oldest in psychology and probably predates the discipline as both Plato and Aristotle engaged with it. At a basic and simple level, the debate asks the question: Are we influenced by that which we inherit through our genes, or are we influenced by our environment? Psychologists, sociologists and philosophers continue to debate this with one side of the argument taking precedence over the other at different periods throughout its history, but the current argument appears to have moved away from the dichotomy, giving both sides equal status, preferring to study their interaction during childhood development. This view is in keeping with my regular discussions with my father in which I parroted the phrase *we are the product of our genes and our environment*, often with reference to my mother, but which of course, also applies to me. Whilst I stand by this view, the percentage impact of each variable on the other eludes me.

There is no doubt that my childhood, as I have described it was unusual. Welsh people are born into a performance culture with singing, poetry and drama being at the heart of school life and the Salvation Army developed this to a significantly greater level, so I was encouraged to perform from a young age. I used to think that I was an extrovert because of this but I now wonder if I am an extroverted introvert or an introvert who learnt to pretend that they are an extrovert as I now often avoid people and shy away from company. From a young age I was required to put aside many of my childhood needs to become mother to my mother, shielding her from the stresses and anxiety of being autistic in a world which was at odds with her neurological makeup. I have described how I was taught, learnt, and devised coping strategies to support her in this and there is no doubt that I have used many of these strategies in my own life. I am aware that these things, combined with my academic and practical knowledge of autism would make me a complex and perhaps challenging candidate for any diagnostician and that they could also influence any diagnosis either way. I have also described a childhood with conflicting and volatile relationships where the expected style of communication was confrontational and aggressive and where I experienced constant criticism. There is no question that this had a negative and damaging effect on some aspects of my communication but most particularly on my self-concept and my self-esteem. I have no doubts that my poor self-esteem was directly related to the constant criticism which I received, particularly as a teenager, and I am still working to remedy this, but my concept of self is a more complex and difficult area for me to explore.

I am not a psychologist, but I understand that the notion of self refers to a mental concept of what one believes they are like as a person. It contributes to the individual's sense of belonging and understanding of how they fit into the world and is achieved through a complex process of development based on how the image of one's self is reflected back to them from social situations and other people. My understanding is that self-image and self-esteem are parts of the self-concept and that they interact with self-knowledge and the social self, to form a complete concept of the individual self. I'm not sufficiently knowledgeable to explain this concept academically but from a personal and retrospective perspective, drawing on decades of self-knowledge, rumination and analysis, I am aware, that the controlling and autocratic parenting style that I received, as described in earlier chapters had a negative effect on both the development of my self-image and my self-esteem, particularly during my teenage years. The images which were reflected back to me as a child, were that I was a tomboy; my father's surrogate son, and through being 'mother to my mother' was a sacrificial carer who put duty and other's needs before my own. Adolescence is a time of rapid physical changes and I'm aware that it is also a significant time in the development of the self-concept, perhaps explaining why this period of development is often viewed by parents as a particularly challenging time. My self-analysis raises no doubt that as a teenager my self-image and self-esteem were adversely affected by my father's negative criticism of both my appearance and my growing sense of independence and perhaps also his description of me as the son which he never had, and that this manifested itself in a fiery temper, earning me the nicknames of 'spitfire' and 'rebel'. I find it interesting that any rebellion did not extend to challenging the sacrificial role that I was both expected and willing to perform, but I recognise that at this time I identified with the reflected image of one who was emotionally sensitive, champion of the underdog, and compassionate: all of which were encouraged by my Christian faith and personal understanding of the teaching and example of

Jesus. Many years of reflection, triggered by my personal tutor's question of 'who are you?', mentioned at the end of Chapter 1 has led me to the understanding that at this period in my life, I had little concept of an independent self, seeing myself only as an attachment or an appendage of others. It seems, as I am writing this, that the balance between nature and nurture is tilted towards nurture but at the same time, I question whether my experience is typical for someone with my life experiences or whether this struggle with the developing self, in relation to others is more typical for autistic people. Either way, I am aware that the development of my self-concept was slow in the making and is still a work in progress, and it has not been without its difficulties.

It is common knowledge that the social naivete of autistic people often results in a vulnerability to abuse in many areas, including finance and relationships and I have also had experience of this. I have known financial hardship, both as a child and an adult but I have no real attachment to money and have no difficulty in giving it away. This has led to me being taken advantage of by people close to me: I have lent money many times without being repaid and I have also taken financial responsibility for others which has been taken for granted and not appreciated. Sharing financial responsibility with my husband for the last forty years has enabled a more managed giving and has protected me from a potential vulnerability to exploitation. More significantly I have experienced sexual abuse. It's said that the introduction of the pill and the Abortion Act in 1967 paved the way for a sexual revolution which led to a sexually permissive society. My memories of this period are that there was a dominant focus on sexual activity and that boys and men thought of little else, but I had suspected that this was always the case. Religion was still very much a part of Welsh life, and the chapels provided the main base for a youth culture where this sexual awareness and openness was frowned upon and suppressed. The effect was one of concealed but rampant sexual activity. I find it difficult to reconcile my sexual experiences during this period, with my current understanding of sexual abuse as whilst I would not make any excuses for, or condone the behaviour of the time, it would be fair to say that most teenagers and young women were used to being sexually harassed and abused. Teenage girls and young women were subject to lewd, suggestive comments and groping on a regular basis and some of us experienced non-consensual sex, long before the term became a familiar concept or part of our vocabulary. For us, sexual harassment and abuse was part of everyday life and we either succumbed to it or fought it off as best we could. I didn't recognise abuse when a fifteen-year-old boy took me, as a ten-year-old girl into a den in waste ground and pulled my underwear down to see my vagina. I simply hit him and then felt embarrassed and humiliated by what he had done. I also recognise that I experienced my first sexual relationship when I was far too young, experiencing no sexual desire at the time but feeling that it was expected of me and that I shouldn't say no. This fortunately was the commencement of a ten-year relationship which protected me from what might otherwise have led to a period of serial sexual relationships or promiscuity. It didn't however protect me from almost being raped at the age of fifteen by two older married men who were mechanics at a garage where I worked during the summer holidays, but fear of discovery was my protector and saviour in this situation. I was also taken advantage of shortly after moving to London, by a colleague who got me (who was previously teetotal) drunk and had non-consensual sex with me. Being unaware of the relationship between alcohol and the concept of consent, I blamed myself at that time for getting drunk and not saying no and I hid the experience from everyone, putting it in the recesses of my memory for many years. It also didn't protect me from the enticement of an emotionally destructive relationship and marriage which was always doomed to failure, and which would cause more damage to my already fragile self-esteem and self-image. Very much later in my life, retrospective self-analysis, supported by counselling enabled me to recognise that my concept of myself as an appendage of others led to my denial of my own needs and a compliance in situations in which I had no desire and felt no control over. This is of course what my personal tutor was seeing in 1973, when he asked me 'Who are you?' but I didn't begin to understand the meaning of this until I became a mother, in 1981, at the age of twenty-eight.

Becoming a mother exorcised the grief and emotional bondage which tied me to an ex-husband who had exhausted me and drained me of all my emotional resources. I was overwhelmed by an intense love for my baby and motherhood became the focus of my being and the centre of my identity. I would have sacrificed everything and willingly walked through fire and died for her, such was the intensity of my emotions. This marked the beginning of a journey to a discovery of self which was independent from others and which is ongoing. It wasn't an easy journey to take: my beautiful baby cried a lot and slept little, and I needed support to recognise that my needs as a single mother were essential in ensuring my ability to take care of her, especially as I was diagnosed with ulcerative colitis when she was just nine months old. It took time to work out how to address both my needs and hers but my growing sense of myself as a separate identity was sufficiently formed for me to enter a balanced and equal relationship with the man who then became my husband, and father of my second daughter, four and a half years later. I intentionally chose a different style of parenting to my parents', vowing that my daughters would be given the freedom to develop their characters with my love, protection, acceptance and guidance but without hindrance, fear or control. Motherhood contributed to an increase in self-image and self-esteem which in turn, with the love and support of my husband has strengthened my belief in myself. My daughters are my proudest achievement and seeing them as wonderful mothers of their own children gives me daily confirmation that I modelled good mothering for them, and that I am also a good mother. It enables me to recognise that I, perhaps am also the confirmation that my mother was a good mother.

Self-image and self-identity are not static and change throughout life. My professional identity as an autism practitioner has dominated my adult life and I am fortunate that the experience of having an autistic mother inadvertently provided me with the skills to be successful in my chosen profession. Determination was one of my mother's greatest attributes, despite her anxieties and fears, and I am grateful that I learned, or inherited this trait from her. I attribute at least some of my professional success to this which has increased my confidence and self-esteem and I believe that I am what I am, and I do what I do, precisely because my mother was autistic. I now find that I, at the age of sixty eight, am in the position of being the oldest member of my family and that in many ways seems unreal. Age and experience have not diminished my passions, but they have mellowed my responses to them. Perhaps that's why I am so comfortable with not knowing the answer to the questions: "what about you Christine? Are you autistic or have you pretended for so long that you don't know?".

Afterword

I have taken the unusual step of writing this short afterward as a means of ensuring that this book meets my stated intention of honouring both my mother and autism. I have written honestly throughout, and at the commencement of this journey didn't anticipate the full extent of the exposure that this would require. I am not embarrassed by the hidden recollections and unwanted happenings that the writing of it has unearthed, but I do recognise that if I am to truly honour autism and my mother then I must clarify some potential difficulties which my revelations have raised. More than anything, I hope that I have not presented my mother as a 'bad mother' because she was autistic, as this is not the case. Mothering in post-industrial society is challenging for all mothers as they struggle to achieve a balance with the various competing roles in their lives, with perfection in all areas being the expectation: a perfection which is unachievable, but which remains the expected standard that we are measured against. Within this framework, as Wenn Lawson pointed out in his Foreword: my mother was a woman of her time. Even more than that, she was an autistic woman of her time and this, and her mothering, needs to be viewed in this context: She was born and raised at a time when neither autism nor Asperger Syndrome were known or understood and she was accepted by her community as being who and what she was, without the need for change. Whilst I applaud that community for its acceptance, I also recognise that the absence of knowledge of autism, together with a different understanding of mental health which was common at that period, inevitably meant that there was no support which could have assisted my mother's social, emotional and educational development and enabled her to understand herself and her needs better. Living successfully in a world that was at odds with her neurological makeup and which caused her high levels of anxiety, consequently depended on her inner resilience and ability to devise her own coping strategies, and she succeeded, and is to be admired in this. She was helped by marrying a man who adored her and looked after her but who was also a man of his time and, like everyone, was affected by his own life experiences. He was shaped by an early life of poverty, hardship, prejudice and discriination, followed by the experience of fighting on the front line during the second world war, but he had no awareness of her neurological difference and the impact that the interaction between this and the dominant society had on her. He, like my mother also had a need to control which caused constant conflict in their marriage, despite originating from different sources. There is no doubt that he loved my mother, but he did not understand her, and he continually tried to change her. There is no blame for this, and it was not his fault: he did his best (as did my mother) with the tools that were available to him at the time. Their best, whilst not being perfect, was good enough and I and my daughters are their legacy and a living testament to that.

I return to Philp Larkin's poem: *This Be The Verse*, in which he succinctly describes the emotional baggage which we all carry with us as a result of our upbringing. This summarises how we are all affected by the parenting which we receive and how we as parents then affect our children. In the poem, Larkin points out that this is not intentional, or specific to individuals, but is an historical accumulation of life experiences and he concludes that the way to ensure an end to this is to not have children. Whilst I found this poem helpful in highlighting the need for me to forgive my parents for their contribution to the emotional baggage which I have carried for much of my life, it also reassures me that this experience is universal. It is not only the experience of children of autistic mothers (or fathers for that matter) but is experienced in differing degrees by all children, of all parents, and many children have had far worse experiences at the hands of neurotypical parents that I had at the hands of mine.

My journey has been a sometimes painful one of discovery, acceptance, and reconciliation and I have learnt much along the way. I have learnt that my mother had many strengths as a parent, precisely because she was autistic: her liking for structure and routine provided stability and solid boundaries for growing children; she was generous without a fault and her generosity was extended to me and my children. I know she and my father would have given their last penny to us if we had needed it and my mother encouraged and developed generosity in me. She was also emotionally resilient; a trait which I strive to attain, and she was also one of the most loyal people I know: she would have walked through fire to defend me (something which I would not have recognised nor understood if I had not had my own daughters), and she was the best shoulder to cry on in times of need.

My journey has taught me that autism is both more simple and more complex than I had realised and that there will always be more to learn. I've learnt that awareness and understanding must always be part of a dynamic process which takes us further along the path to full acceptance and that this will be a constant work in progress until it is fully achieved. I'm both angered and saddened when I see and hear reports of the ill treatment of autistic people in psychiatric hospitals and I despair of the slow progress that has been made in the seventy-seven years since Kanner first made us aware of autism. Telling my mother's story has highlighted both the setbacks and the progression that have been made since then. My mother was protected by my father and her community from the medicalisation of autism, which is prevalent in the twenty first century, so she was not subjected to attempts to treat or cure her from a condition, but was accepted without prejudice and discrimination. Whilst there were many positive aspects to this, and I am thankful for them, it has to be said that acceptance without understanding provided little support or helpful practical strategies which could have improved my mother's understanding of herself and supported her social and emotional development, and our family life. Understanding would also have enabled others, especially my father to live a life more in harmony with her. We now have awareness and an increased understanding of autism, so that twenty first century autistic mothers no longer have my mother's experience, but I am saddened and disappointed that this has taken the medicalised route which has hindered full acceptance, and negatively impacted on professional practice. My mother experienced acceptance without a label and understanding of autism, but acceptance is no longer the experience of most autistic people, despite society's increased awareness of autism. The medicalised approach to autism, which prefers to focus on changing and normalising autistic people has unfortunately been a major setback to true acceptance.

Unlike Larkin, I believe that patterns can be broken and that it is possible for parents to not repeat the historical mistakes of the past, so I do not advocate his solution of childlessness. Parenthood is challenging and throughout history mothers have been blamed and vilified for the failures of society to meet the needs of its children. The loss of the extended family has been accompanied by the loss of support networks which are not easily replaced by paid professionals, however caring and well intentioned they may be, and many mothers are left struggling to balance their responsibilities. Autistic girls grow up to be autistic women, many of whom become autistic mothers. They may mother their children differently to many other mothers but there is no wrong in this and they too can be good mothers. Like all mothers everywhere, they need support, understanding and acceptance in providing what is in my mind one of the most important and rewarding roles that there is.

It is my hope that this book has gone some way to enabling that.

Glossary of terms used

Asperger Syndrome	I have chosen not to use this term, preferring to use the more inclusive term autism, to refer to the whole autism spectrum. On the few occasions it is found in the text, it is used to refer to a diagnostic term or is in relation to a quotation from others. Asperger Syndrome is no longer used as a diagnostic label and is not included in the DSM V criteria for Autistic Spectrum Disorders.
Autism	I have chosen to use this term throughout the book as it is the most inclusive word to describe what is also called the autism spectrum as it does not differentiate according to ability. Autism is increasingly becoming the preferred term of autistic people.
Autistic people	I have chosen to use identity first language as opposed to person first

language ie: 'people with autism', as autistic people tell us that autism is a fundamental part of their identity which cannot be removed. It is also the most inclusive and linguistically correct term to use as 'people with autism' indicates autism as an addition to the norm.

AWOL	This is an anacronym for the military term' Absent without leave'. It indicates a person's absence without permission.
Neurotypical	This word is used to describe the majority neurotype. Like Wenn Lawson, I view the term 'neurodiverse' as simply meaning all neurotypes of which autism is just one.
Obsessed	I choose not to use this word because of the negative connotations that it conveys. When I have used it in the text, it has been intentional, either as a means of indicating how my language use has changed over time or in order to convey negativity.
Obsessions /s	See above.
Suffer	I do not use this word in relation to autism as it has a negative meaning which indicates something which has to be endured. When it is used, it indicates a personal suffering.

About the Author

Christine Breakey is an Autism Advocate; an Autism Support Tutor and Founder of Spectrum First Ltd. She's worked with autistic people since 1972 in a variety of settings and is passionate about autism and challenging discrimination. She loves writing and is author of The Autism Spectrum and Further Education, and co-author of Access and Inclusion for Children with Autistic Spectrum Disorders, both published by Jessica Kingsley Publishers.

Printed in Great Britain
by Amazon